MY FIRST ORIGAMI BOOK

with 80 Sheets of Origami Paper + How-To Videos

RITA FOELKER

Dover Publications, Garden City, New York

This Dover edition, first published in 2025, is a new English translation of *La Mia Prima Scuola di Origami* by Rita Foelker, published by NuiNui, Vercelli, Italy, in 2022.

ISBN-13: 978-0-486-85562-2
ISBN-10: 0-486-85562-7

Printed in China
85562701 2025
www.doverpublications.com

Frame the QR code included with each project to access a video tutorial!

To print the colored paper templates found inside the book, use this link: www.nuinui.ch/upload/scuola-origami.pdf

Credits
Origami paper patterns:
freepik.com - freepik.com/Macrovector - freepik.com/Pikisuperstar - freepik.com/Starline
freepik.com/Renata-s - freepik.com/vector-corp - freepik.com/Lesyaskripak - freepik.com/Mokoland

p.18: freepik.com/rawpixel.com - p.16 and p.19: freepik.com

TEXTS, IMAGES, AND VIDEOS
RITA FOELKER

PHOTOGRAPHS
PAOLO BIANO

Contents

Chapter 2

Chapter 3

Chapter 4

Chapter 5

Chapter 6

Chapter 7

Introduction

What origami means to me

Origami has been part of my life since I was a child. But it was about 35 years ago that I truly fell in love with this art. I started buying books, studying different models, and folding paper into all sorts of shapes. Over time, I discovered that origami offers challenges for everyone—some folds are simple, while others are more complex. What really matters is finding clear instructions to follow, no matter the difficulty of the pattern.

The Internet became a valuable resource, helping me dive deeper into the language of origami diagrams. I realized that knowing the BASIC, or BASE FOLDS, made learning so much easier.

With all this knowledge and experience, I decided to create something special: a book called *My First Origami Book*. I hope it brings you as much joy as it has brought me. Whether you're folding alone, with friends, or teaching others, may you find delight in transforming simple paper into beautiful objects, decorations, and toys.

Rita Foelker

Origami art and technique

Paper was invented in China, and its production techniques were then spread to several other countries by Buddhist monks. Among these countries was Japan, where, according to scholars, the first origami folds appeared in the 7th century.

In the 8th century, origami became part of Shinto[1] ceremonies. At that time, there were extremely strict rules about folding paper. Folding was a way of honoring the spirits of the trees that were used in making the paper.

Recreational origami dates back to the Heian period (794–1185 CE), with records of paper folded into the shapes of herons, boats, and dolls. In the Edo period (1603–1868 CE), more than 70 models were created, including the famous "tsuru" (crane).

The first book that contained instructions on how to make origami was published in 1797, and is called *Hiden Senbazuru Orikata* ("Secret to Folding One Thousand Cranes").

In the 19th century, Friedrich Fröbel (1782–1852), a German educator and the inventor of kindergarten, introduced paper folding to students as a purposeful educational activity.

However, it was only in the 20th century that the art of origami spread throughout Europe, thanks to popular origami instructions written by Japan's Isao Honda (1888–1975) and Spain's Miguel de Unamuno (1864–1936).

Origami, meaning "folding" (ori) "paper" (kami), can be used in many ways to create wonderful objects. They can be given as gifts, or used as decorations for parties and special occasions. Folding paper can be a recreational activity, and it can be used as an educational tool for all ages.

Today, a wide variety of books in many languages promote the art of origami worldwide. National and international origami events are held every year. And thanks to the Internet and social networks, the work of paper folders can be widely shared and appreciated.

[1] Shinto is an ancient Japanese religion.

Origami and its many benefits

Widespread as a hobby but recognized as an art, origami today is used not only in education, but also for recreation and decoration. This ancient art is particularly valued for its ability to stimulate concentration, mental order, and creativity, in addition to helping the development of spatial vision, hand-eye coordination, and artistic sense.

Mathematicians, computer scientists, and engineers have discovered that the knowledge and skills necessary to make origami can help solve many problems in their areas of research. Origami concepts are also applied in the fields of space technology, molecular chemistry, and industry.

Origami symbols for beginners

A SHORT GUIDE OF THE MOST COMMON SYMBOLS

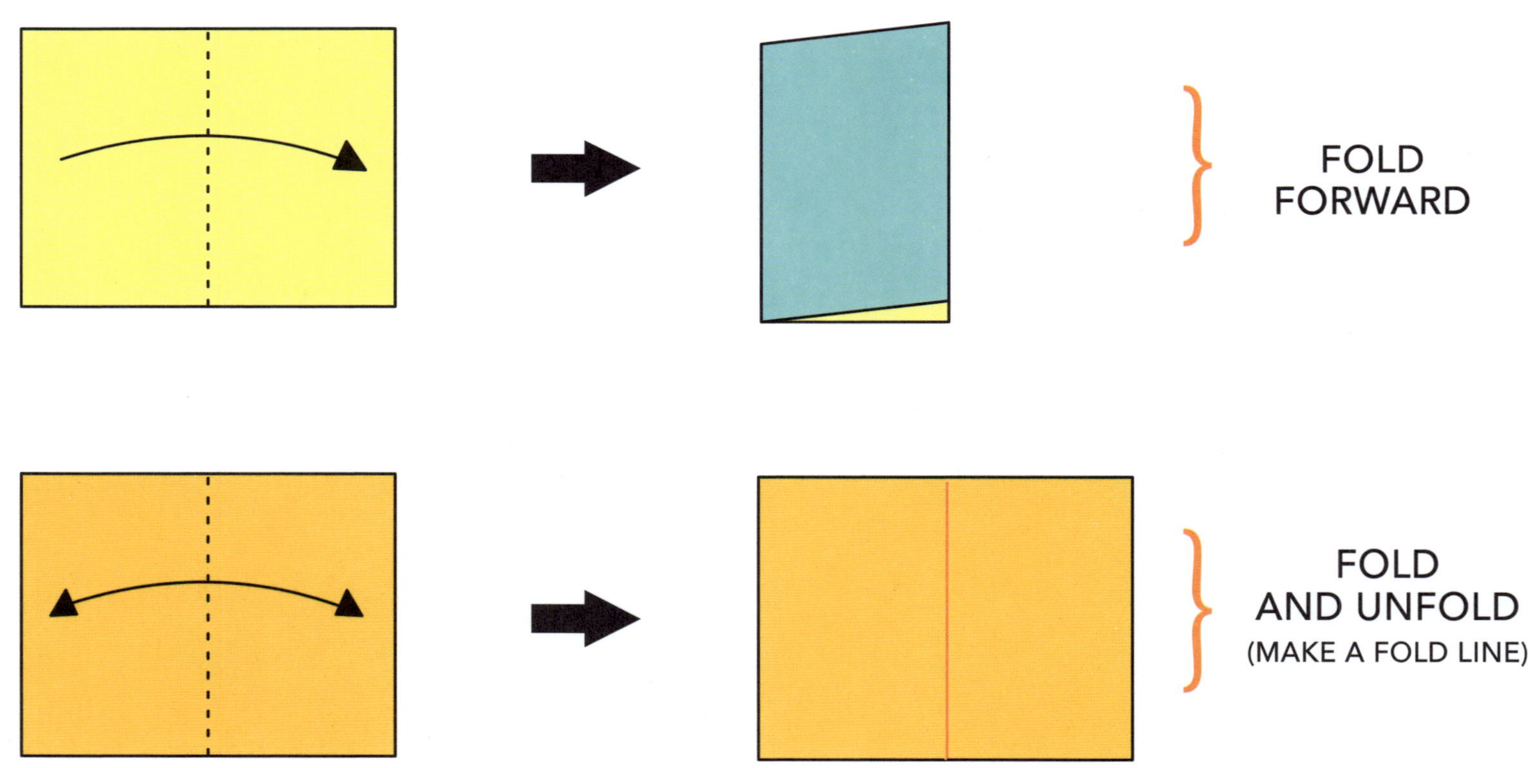

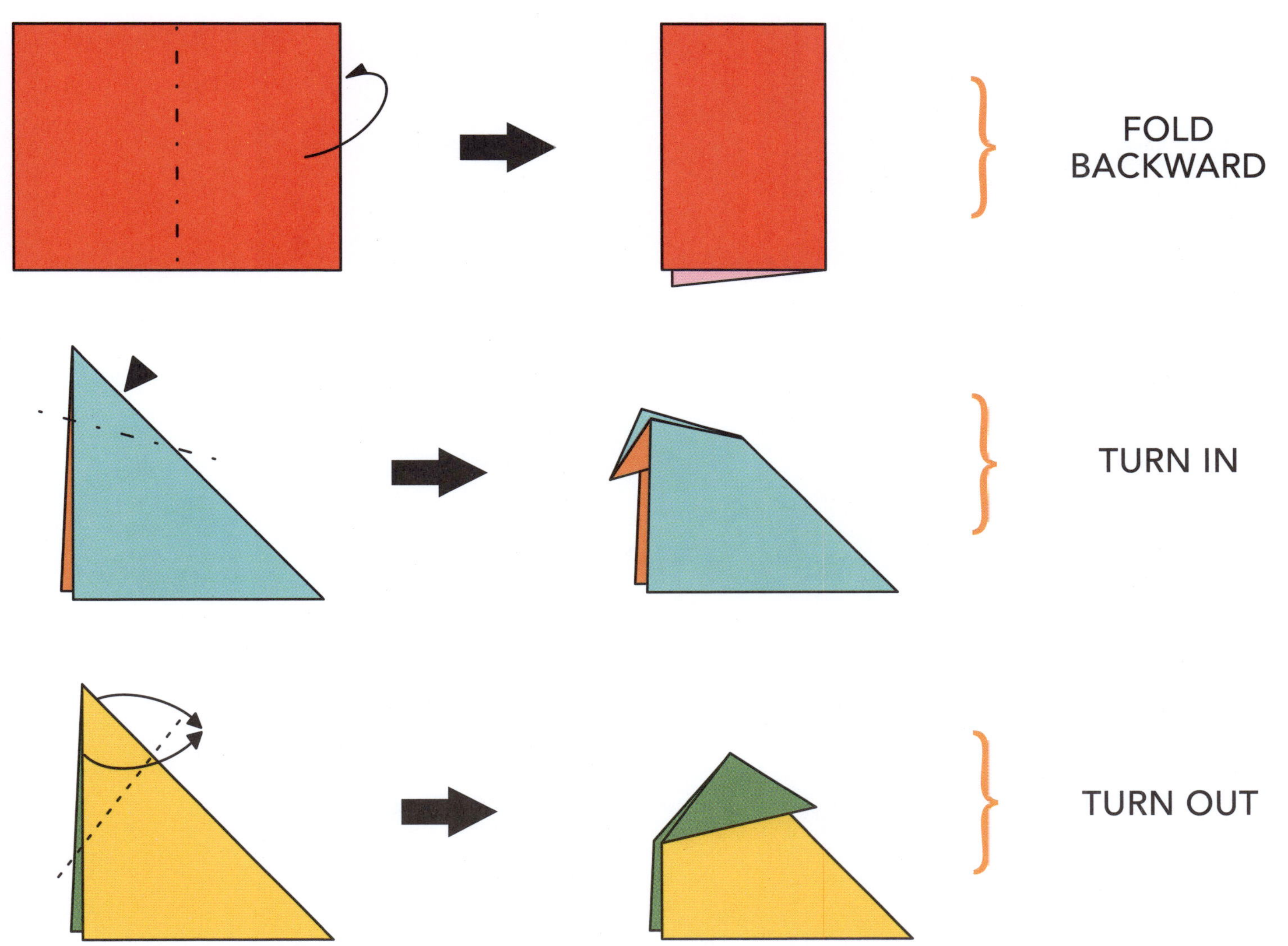
FOLD
BACKWARD
TURN IN
TURN OUT

ZIGZAG FOLD

FLIP
THE PAPER
REPEAT ON THE
OTHER SIDE
OPEN
TURN
THE PAPER
CUT
ZOOMED IMAGE

What kind of paper should I use?

There is excellent Korean and Japanese paper specially designed for origami. These papers are sold at specialty shops or sites. (You can find many varieties on the Internet.)

However, you can also find good, everyday paper in stationery shops, such as offset or uncoated paper, usually used in inkjet or laser printers. You can also print a pattern, suitable for the model you are going to fold, and get the exact result you want.

Even wrapping paper with a decorated side can create extraordinary effects, but only a few types are suitable for origami. To see if the wrapping paper will work, fold one corner and go over the crease with your finger or fingernail. If the paper stays folded, it's perfect. If it pops up quickly, it just won't work.

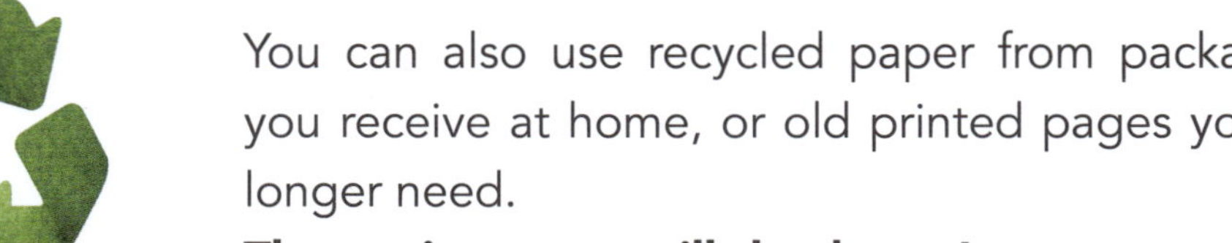

You can also use recycled paper from packaging you receive at home, or old printed pages you no longer need.
The environment will thank you!

Some time ago, I had printed a few music scores and thought of using these to make origami boxes. The end result was quite stunning!

A few helpful tips before you begin

HERE ARE SOME TIPS TO HELP YOU GET BETTER RESULTS.

1. Pay attention to the measurements of the paper. A square must have all four sides exactly the same length; otherwise, the folds will be uneven, jeopardizing the final result.

2. When folding, be very precise. If two sides of the paper have to overlap, they must fit together as exactly as possible.

3. Use your finger or fingernail to help make each fold. It is important that you do this. Otherwise, the finished piece won't have "crisp" lines and it won't look polished.

4. Take as much time as you need with the step you're working on, as if it were the most important step of all.

5. Just keep at it. If your first attempt is unsuccessful, don't give up. No one is perfect when they first try folding paper. Try and try again. You'll see that the more you practice, the better you'll get at the art of origami.

Basic origami folds

Most traditional origami models are made from bases, or basic folds. Learning the basic folds is an important step in making the more complex models.

So let's learn how to make some basic shapes and the beautiful models you can create using them.

In this book you will discover:

THE KITE BASE

THE DIAMOND BASE

THE FISH BASE

THE BOOK BASE

Some origami books and websites begin by asking you to start from a certain base. Once you know these, you will be able to make lots of models you find online and in books!

The projects in this book have different levels of difficulty. Follow the symbols below, and start with the "beginner" projects. As you become more and more comfortable folding paper, you can advance to the "intermediate" projects.

CHAPTER 1

EVERY YEAR ON MAY 5, JAPANESE CHILDREN CELEBRATE "KODOMO NO HI" (CHILDREN'S DAY) BY FOLDING AND WEARING PAPER SAMURAI HELMETS, CALLED "KABUTO."

ONCE YOU'VE LEARNED TO FOLD THE HELMET BASE, YOU CAN USE IT TO CREATE MANY OTHER TRADITIONAL ORIGAMI.

n°1

THE HELMET BASE

Paper included

USE A SQUARE SHEET OF PAPER

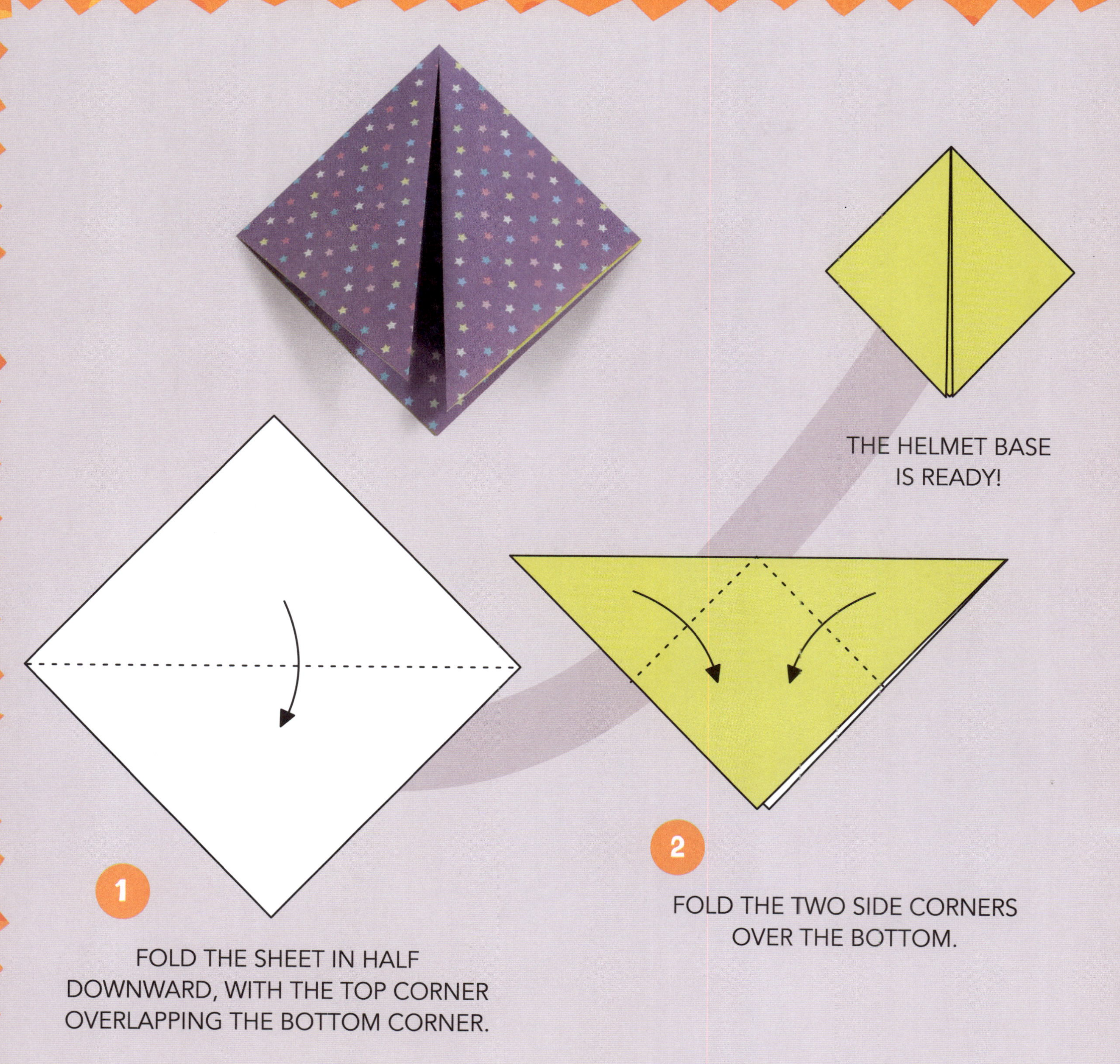

1

FOLD THE SHEET IN HALF DOWNWARD, WITH THE TOP CORNER OVERLAPPING THE BOTTOM CORNER.

2

FOLD THE TWO SIDE CORNERS OVER THE BOTTOM.

nº 2

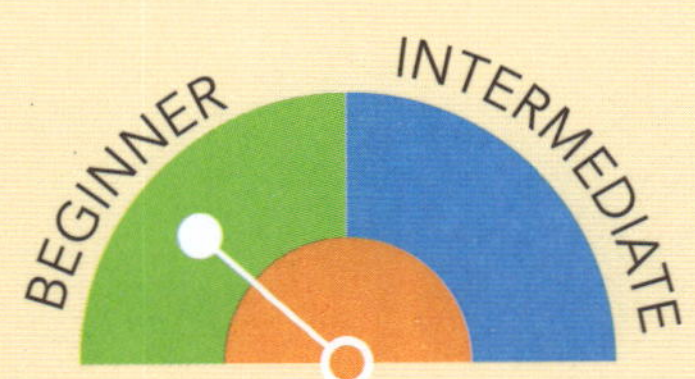

Paper included

THE SAMURAI HELMET

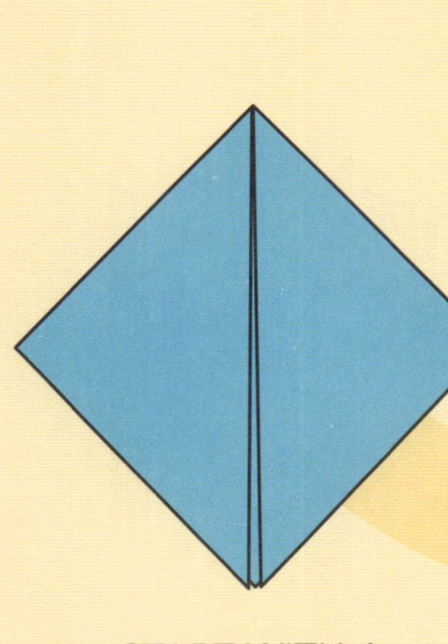

START WITH A HELMET BASE.

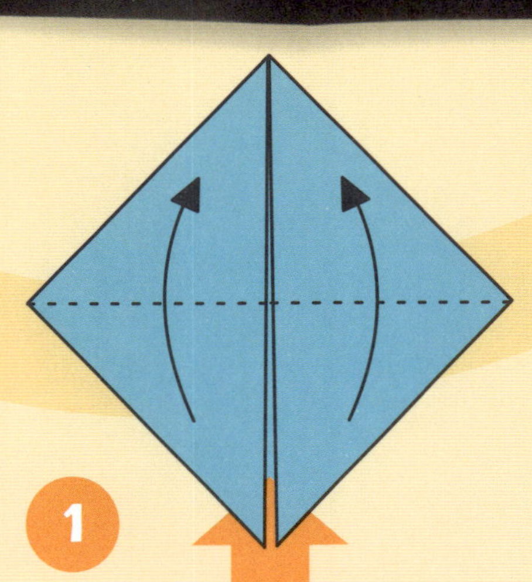

1

FOLD THE TWO LOWER ENDS UPWARD.

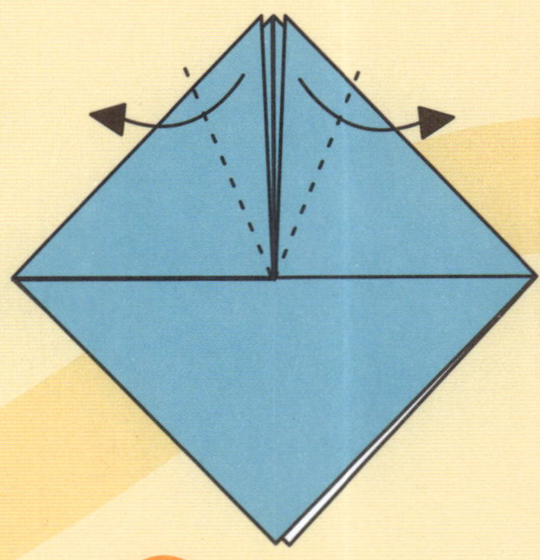

2

OPEN BOTH ENDS OUTWARD.

THE SAMURAI HELMET IS READY!

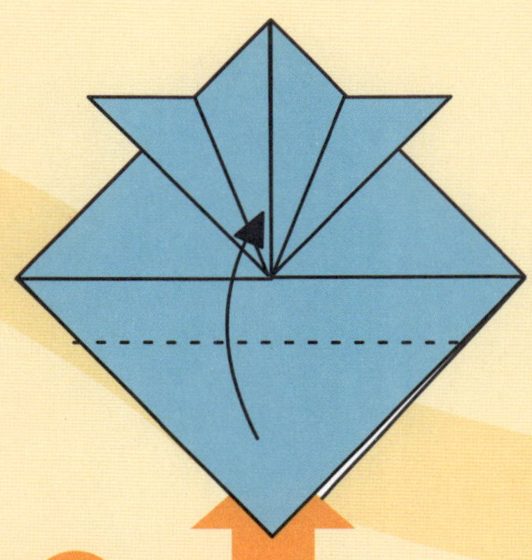

3

FLAP UP THE LOWER LAYER, AND FOLD AS SHOWN IN THE IMAGE.

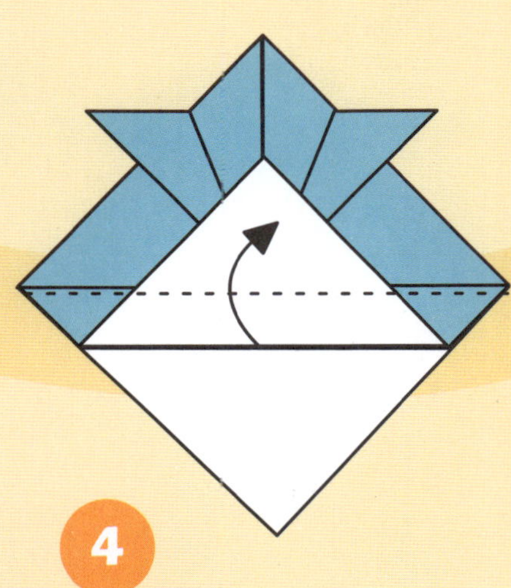

4

FOLD THE FRONT FLAP UPWARD.

5

FOLD THE OTHER BOTTOM LAYER, AND TUCK IT INSIDE THE HELMET.

n°3

⇧ Paper included

THE CICADA

START WITH A HELMET BASE.

180°

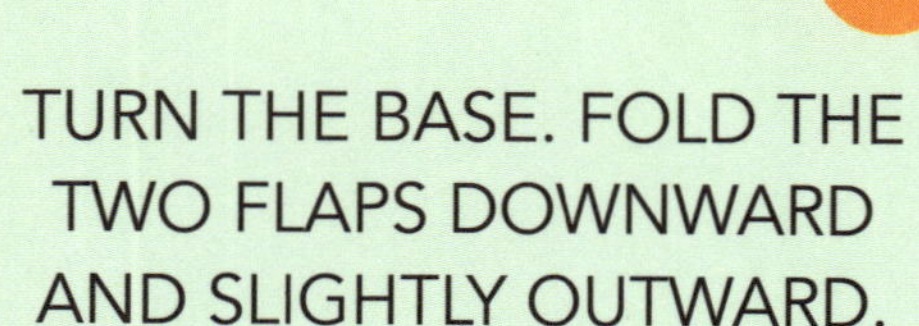

1

TURN THE BASE. FOLD THE TWO FLAPS DOWNWARD AND SLIGHTLY OUTWARD.

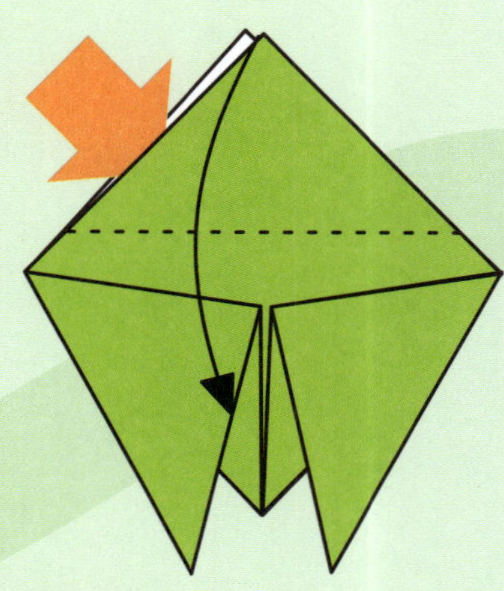

2

OPEN THE UPPER SECTION AND FOLD ONE LAYER DOWN.

THE CICADA IS READY!

6

FOLD THE TWO UPPER CORNERS FORWARD.

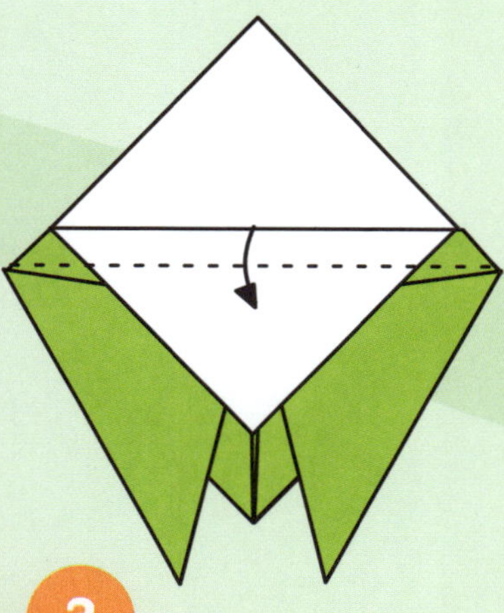

3

FOLD A THIN STRIP OF PAPER OVER IT AS SHOWN.

4

FOLD BACK BOTH SIDES.

5

ALSO FOLD BACK THE UPPER END.

n°4

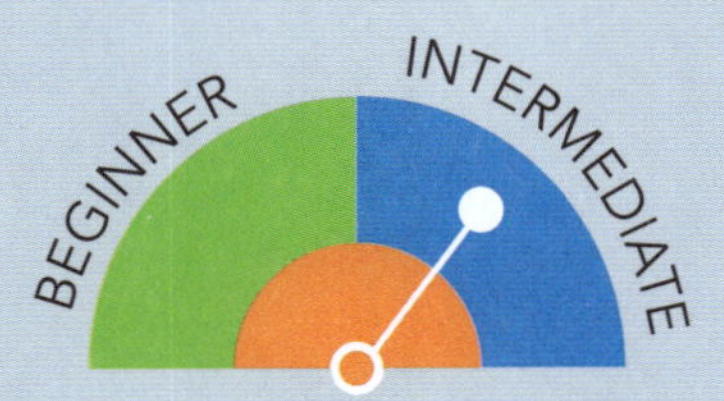

⇧ Paper included

THE GOLDFISH

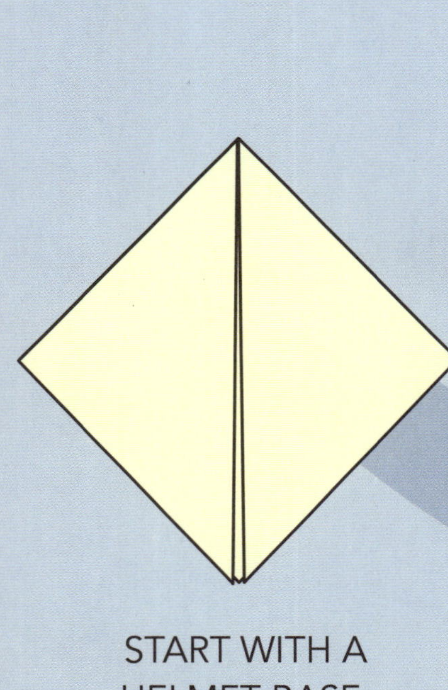

START WITH A HELMET BASE.

1

FOLD THE TWO LOWER ENDS UPWARD.

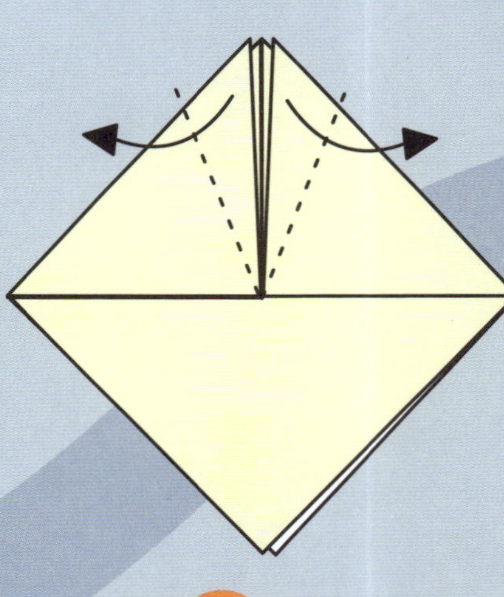

2

OPEN BOTH ENDS OUTWARD.

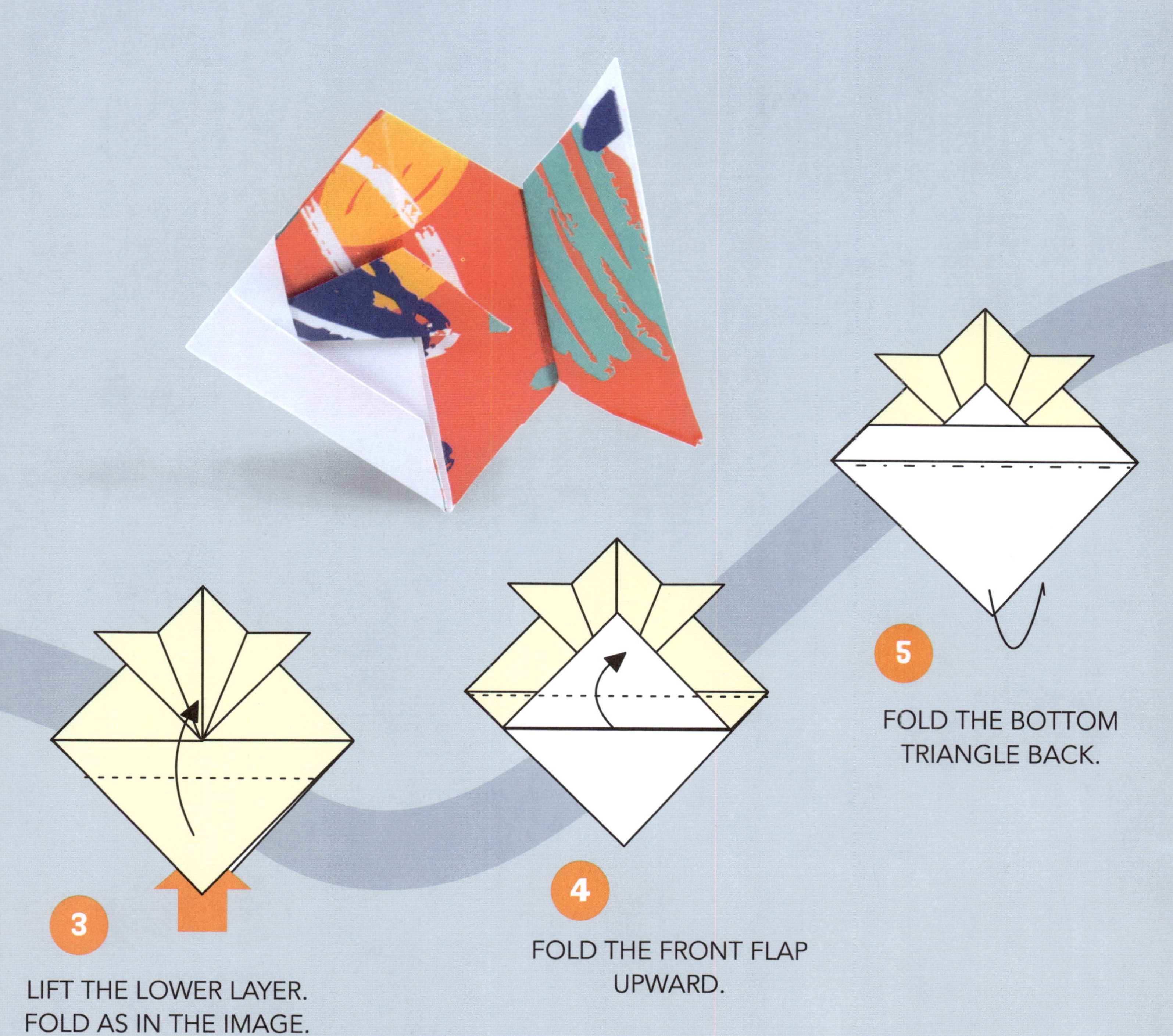

3

LIFT THE LOWER LAYER.
FOLD AS IN THE IMAGE.

4

FOLD THE FRONT FLAP
UPWARD.

5

FOLD THE BOTTOM
TRIANGLE BACK.

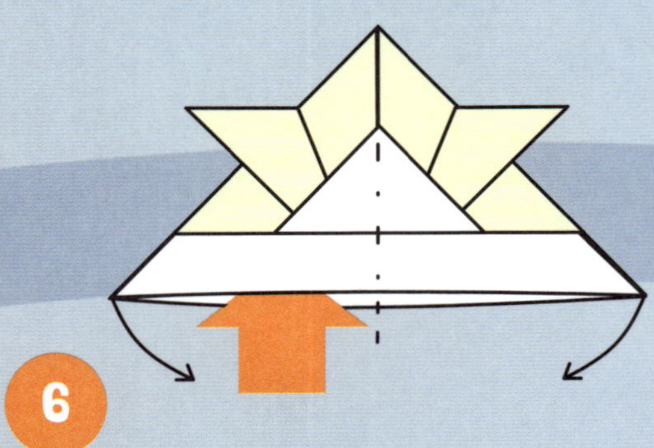

6

FLATTEN EVERYTHING
AND JOIN THE TWO
LOWER ENDS AS SHOWN.

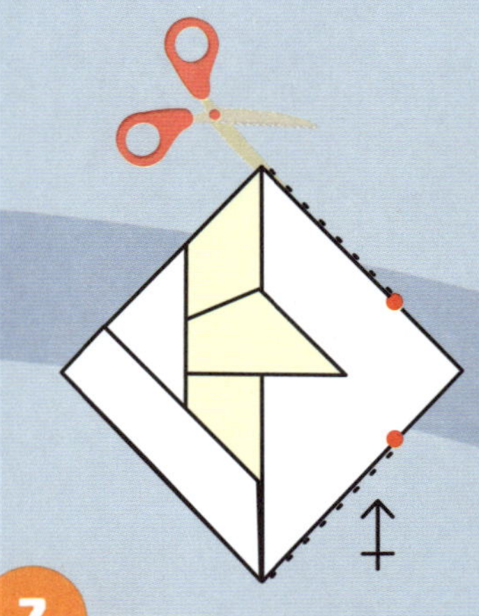

7

CUT ALONG THE EDGES
TO THE RED POINTS
AS ILLUSTRATED.

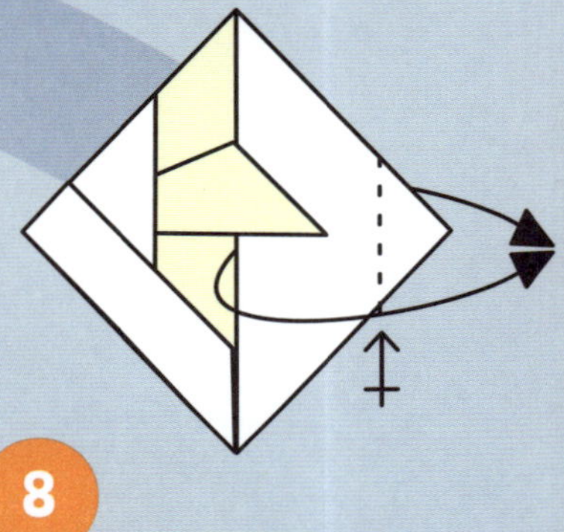

8

LIFT THE FLAP AND
FOLD IT ALONG THE
DOTTED LINE. REPEAT ON
THE REVERSE SIDE.

THE GOLDFISH IS READY!

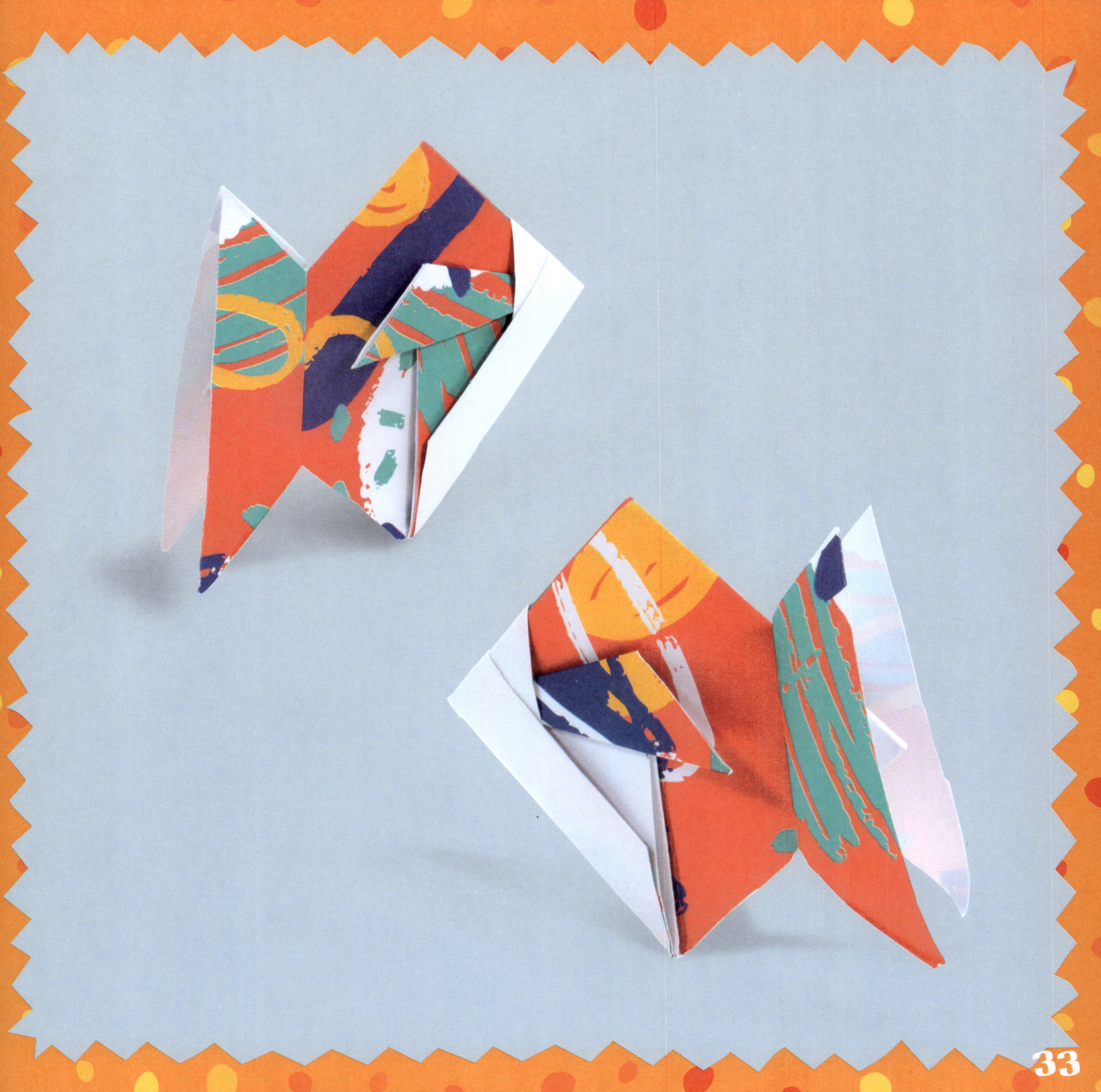

CHAPTER 2

IT LOOKS LIKE A DOOR AND IS VERY EASY TO FOLD. THE DOOR BASE CAN BE USED TO CREATE A 3-DIMENSIONAL BOX.

IT REALLY IS
INCREDIBLE!

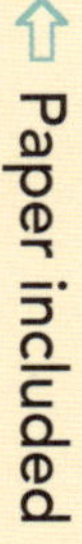

nº 5 THE DOOR BASE

USE A SQUARE SHEET OF PAPER

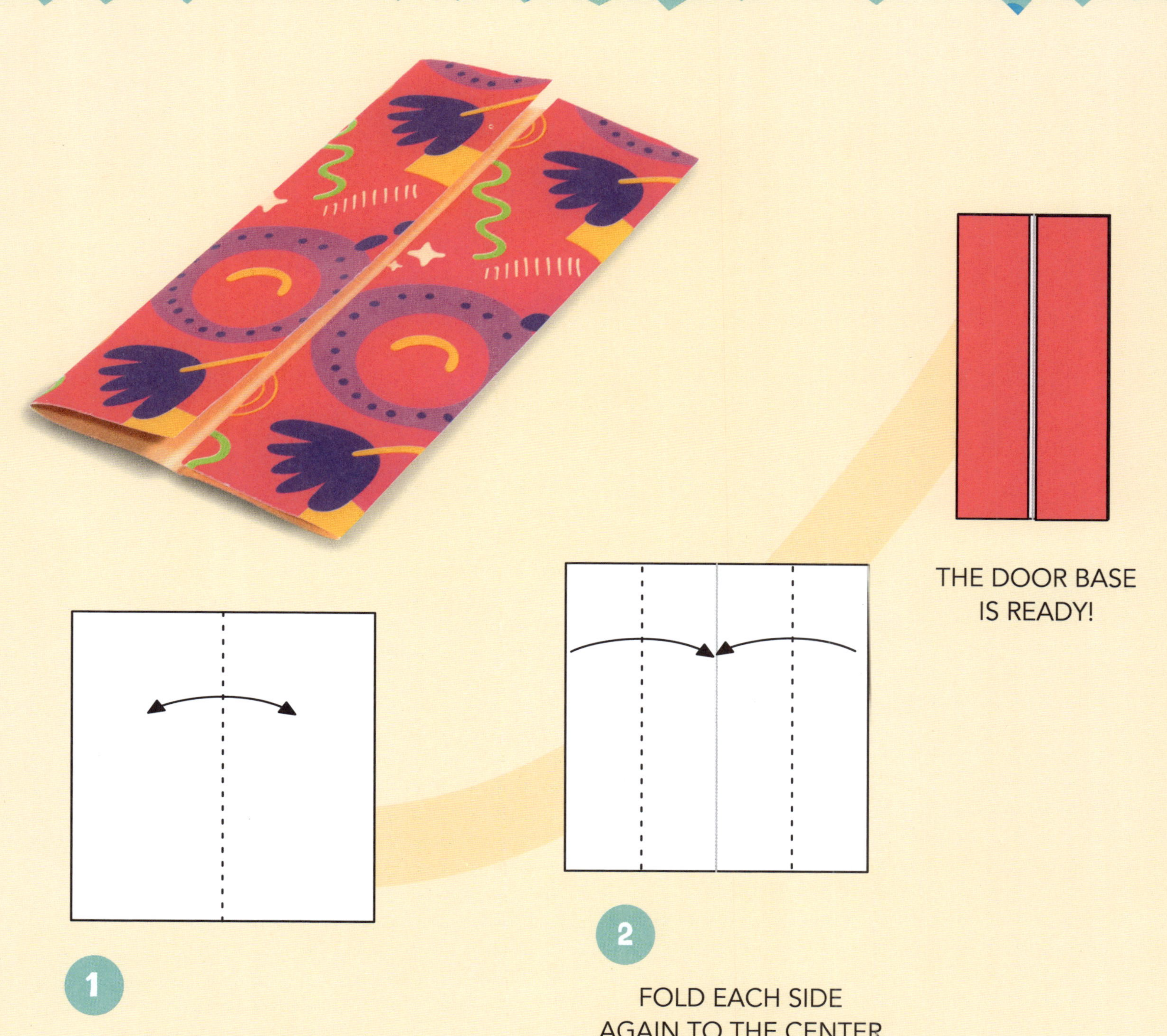

FOLD EACH SIDE
AGAIN TO THE CENTER
CREASE LINE.

FOLD THE SHEET
IN HALF, RIGHT SIDE TO
LEFT SIDE, AND OPEN.

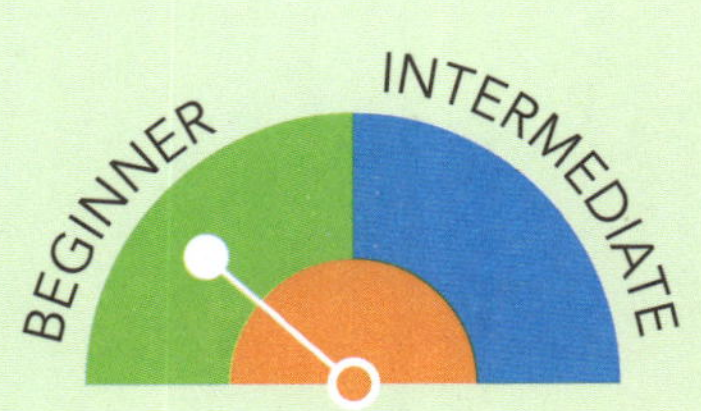

⇧ Paper included

nº 6

THE RECTANGLE BOX

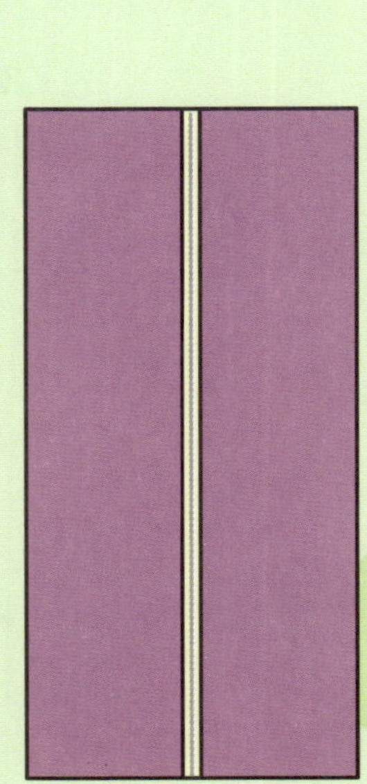

START WITH THE DOOR BASE.

1

FOLD TWO THIN STRIPS FROM THE CENTER OUTWARD.

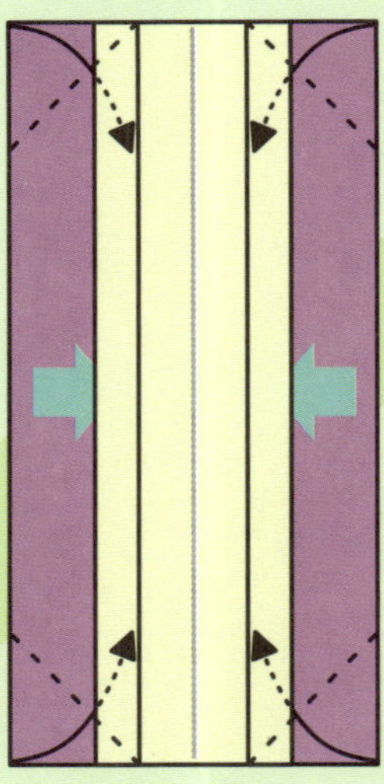

2

LIFT THE FLAPS AND FOLD THE FOUR CORNERS. TUCK THEM UNDER THE FLAPS.

SOMETHING MORE:

YOU CAN ALSO MAKE THIS BOX WITH A RECTANGULAR SHEET OF PAPER.

IF YOU FOLD ANOTHER SMALLER SHEET (3–5 MM ON THE SHORTER SIDE), YOU CAN MAKE A BOX WITH A LID.

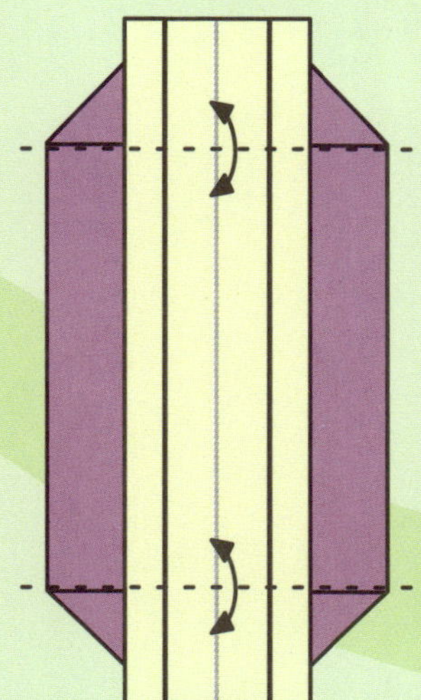

3

FOLD TWICE ALONG THE BASE OF THE TRIANGLES.

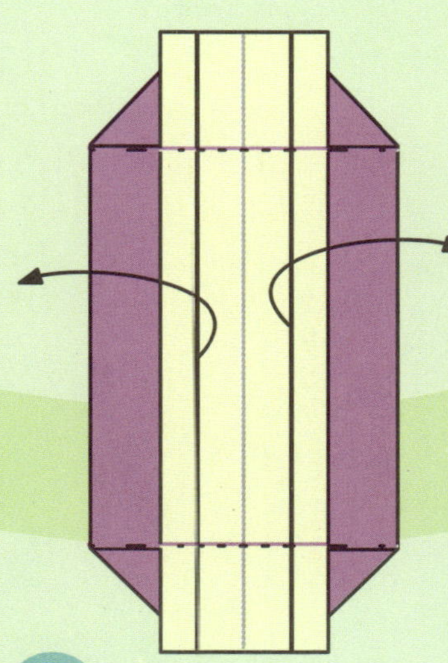

4

OPEN AT THE CENTER AND SHAPE THE CORNERS.

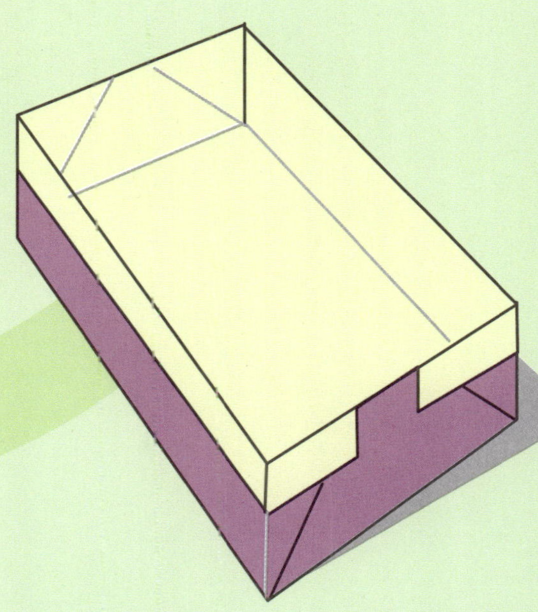

THE RECTANGULAR BOX IS READY!

CHAPTER 3

THE ORGAN BASE IS THE STARTING BASE FOR A NUMBER OF ORIGAMI MODELS.

I CHOSE THE PIANO AMONG THESE BECAUSE IT IS VERY FUN!

n°7

THE ORGAN BASE

⇧ Paper included

USE A SQUARE SHEET OF PAPER

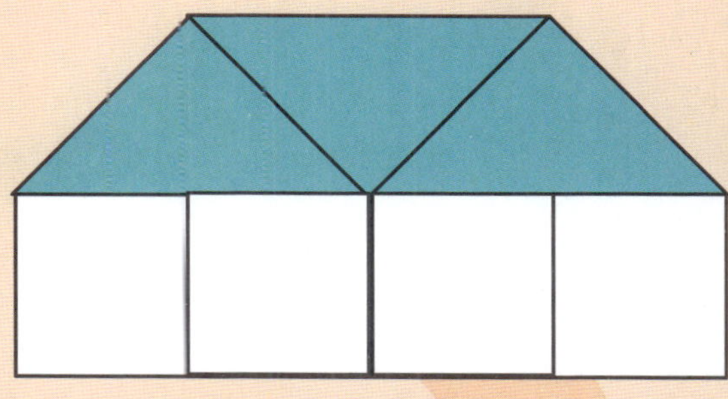

THE ORGAN BASE
IS READY!

4

OPEN BOTH SIDES.
FLATTEN THE TRIANGLES
IN THE UPPER PART.

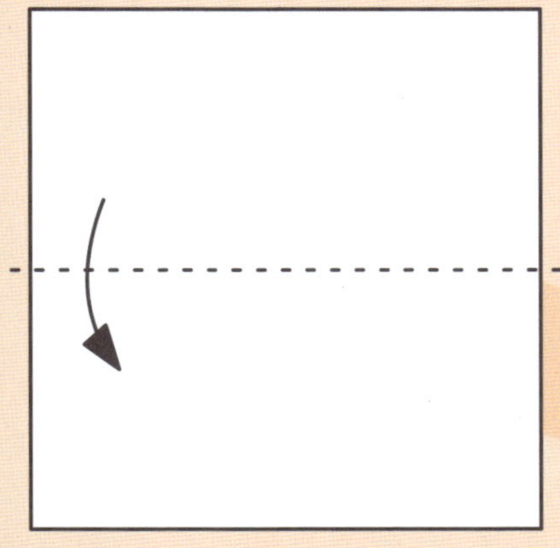

1

FOLD THE SHEET
IN HALF. FOLD THE
TOP OVER THE
BOTTOM, AND OPEN.

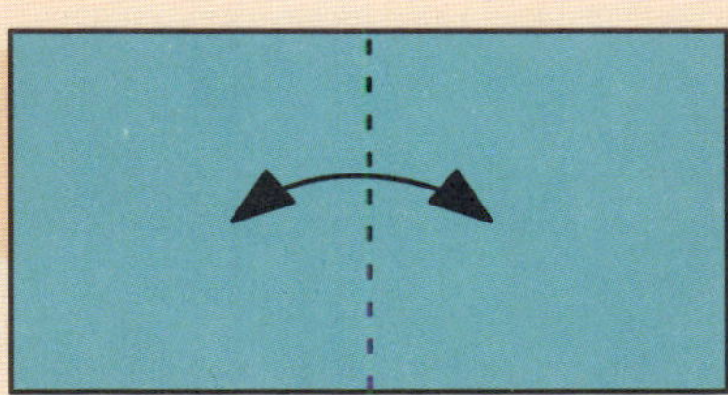

2

FOLD IN HALF,
SIDE TO SIDE, AND OPEN.

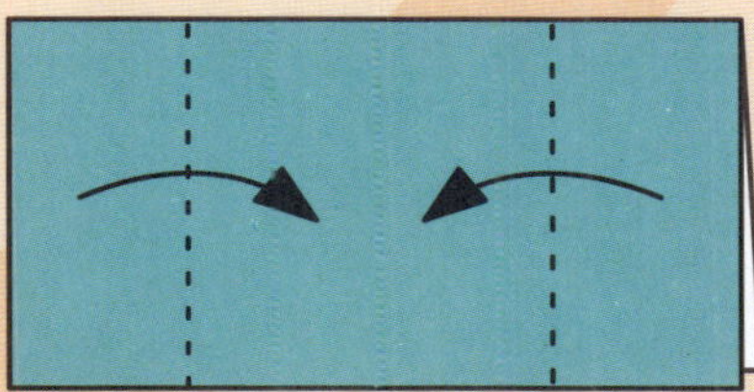

3

FOLD BOTH SIDES
TO THE CENTER
CREASE LINE.

nº 8

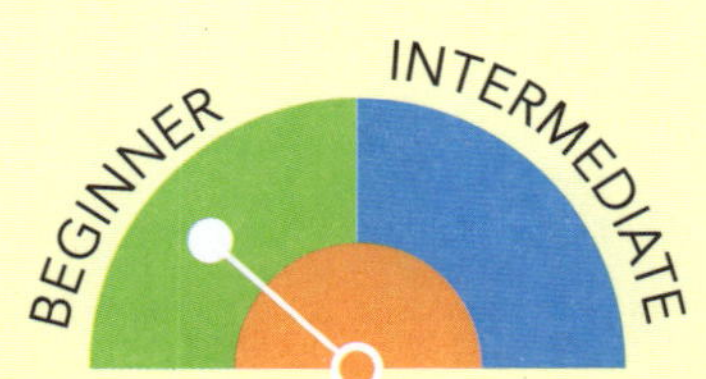

⇧ Paper included

THE PIANO

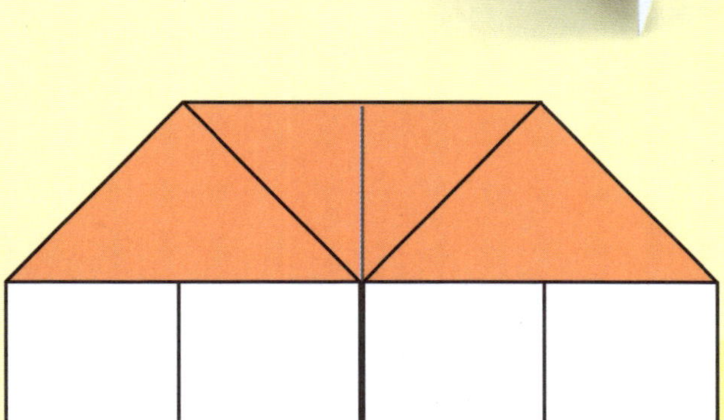

START AT THE
BASE OF THE ORGAN.

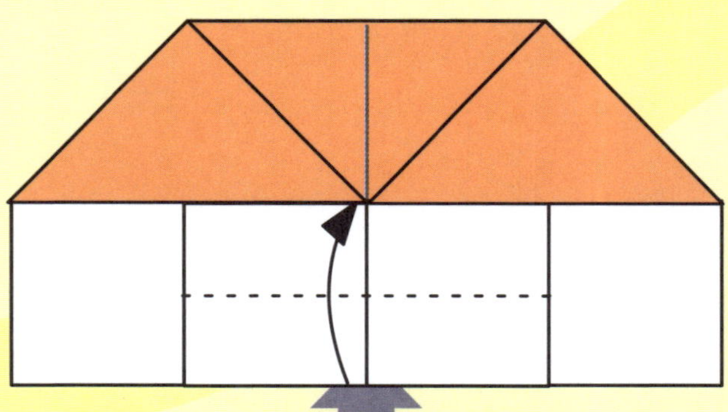

1

FOLD THE FRONT PART
TOWARD THE CENTER.

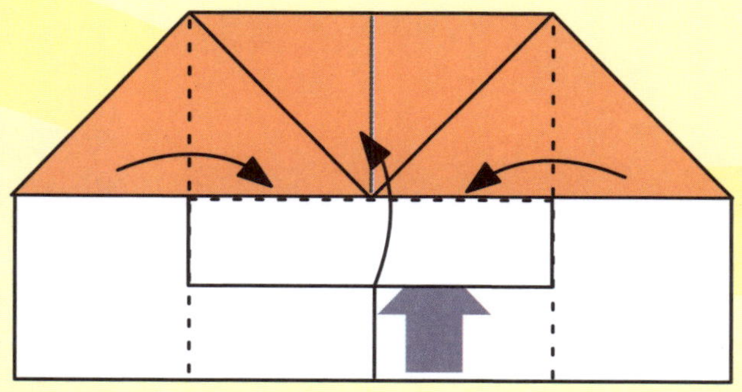

2

FOLD THE TWO SIDES TOWARD THE CENTER AND LIFT UP THE FRONT PART.

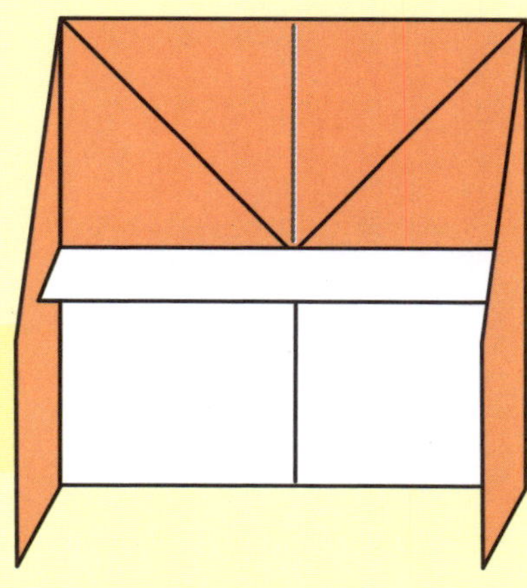

THE PIANO IS READY!

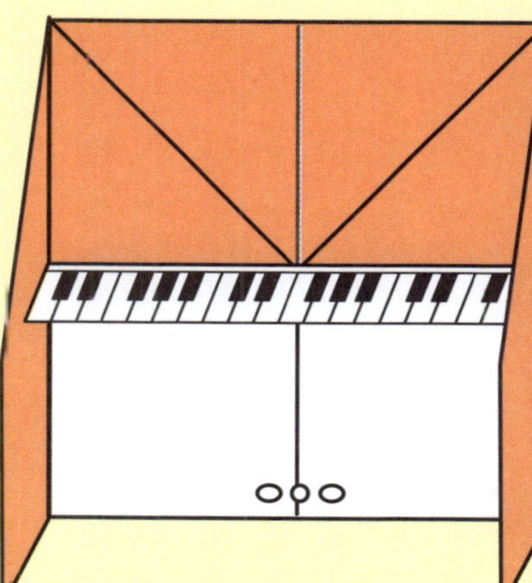

DRAW ON THE KEYS AND PEDALS.

CHAPTER 4

HERE IS THE KITE BASE!

NAMED AFTER ITS SHAPE, THE KITE BASE IS THE FOUNDATION OF MANY ORIGAMI MODELS. ONCE YOU LEARN THIS BASE, YOU WILL START FROM THIS POINT MANY TIMES OVER.

THE KITE BASE

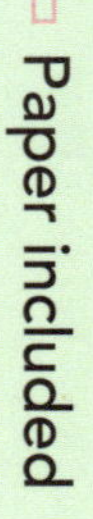

USE A SQUARE SHEET OF PAPER

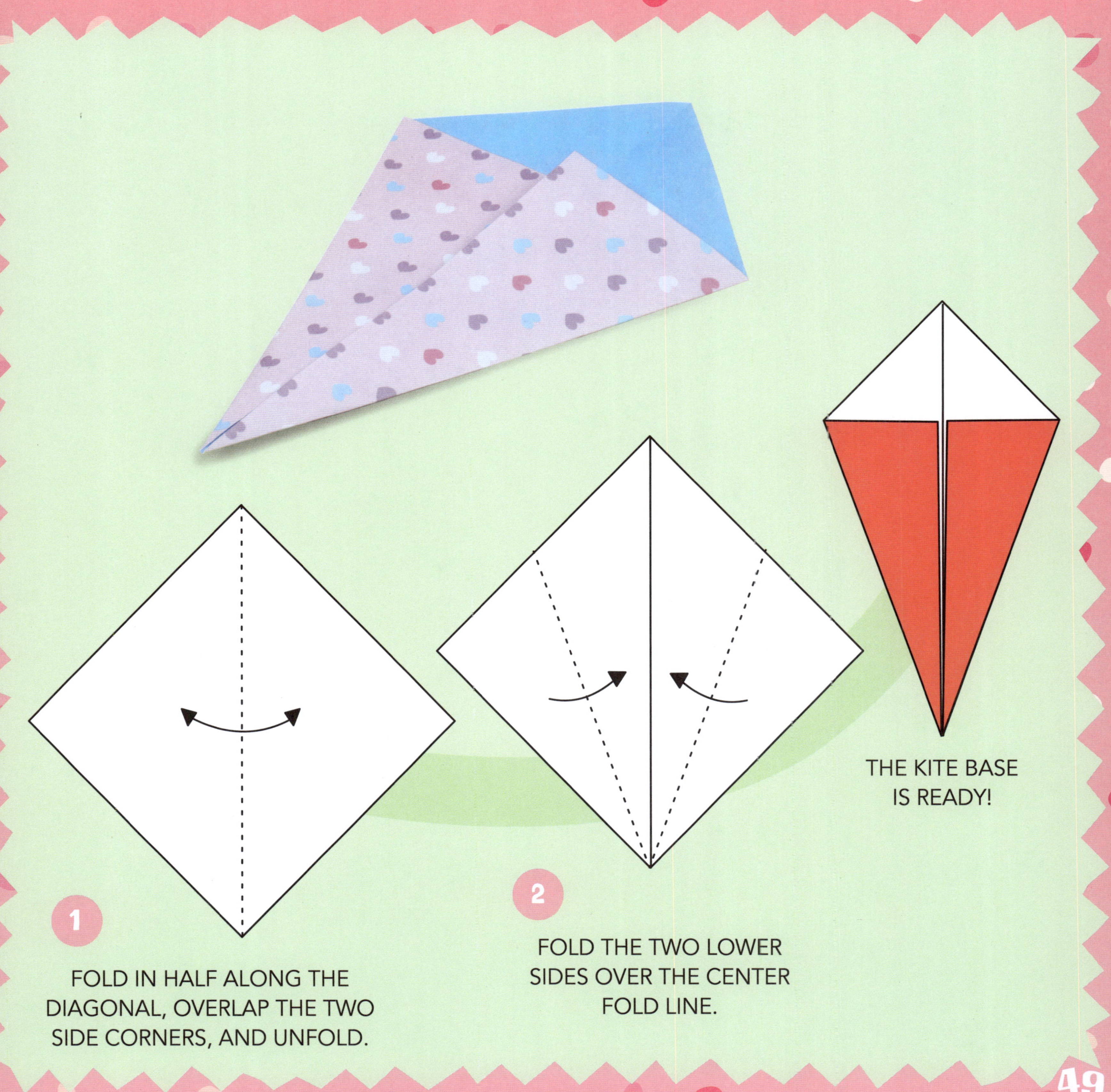
THE KITE BASE
IS READY!
1
FOLD IN HALF ALONG THE
DIAGONAL, OVERLAP THE TWO
SIDE CORNERS, AND UNFOLD.
2
FOLD THE TWO LOWER
SIDES OVER THE CENTER
FOLD LINE.

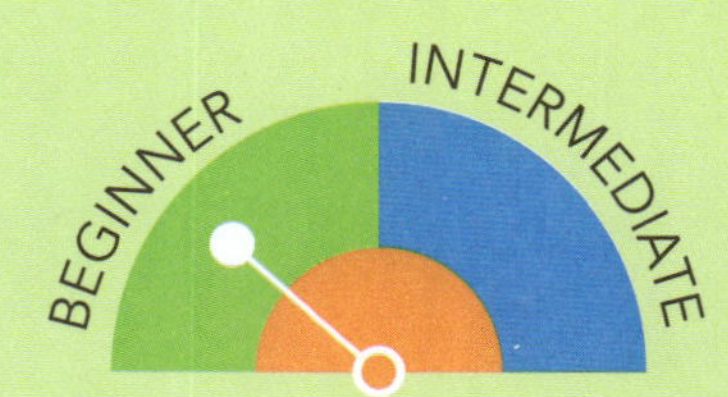

Paper included

THE PINE TREE

START WITH A KITE BASE.

180°

1

ROTATE THE BASE.

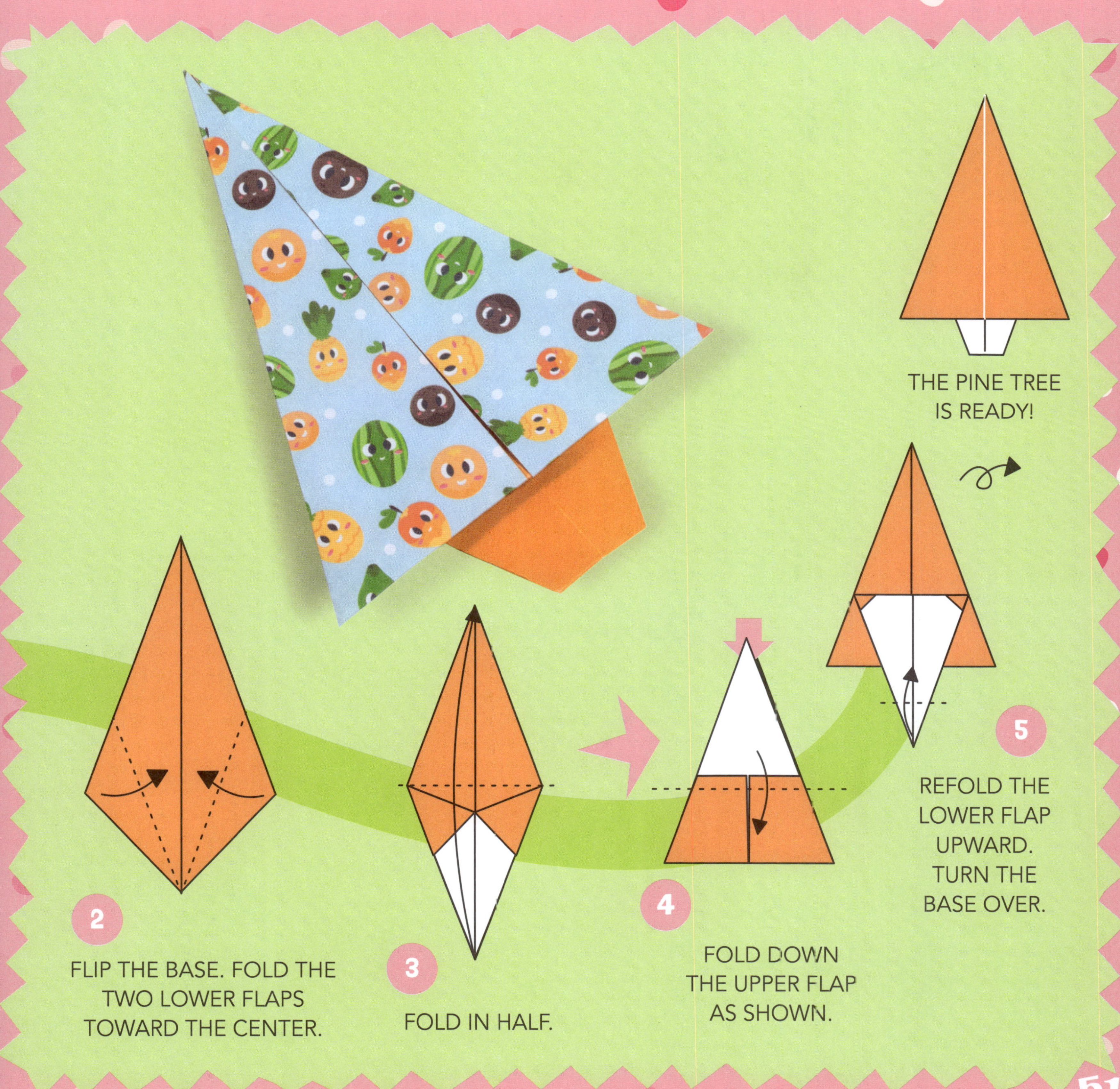
THE PINE TREE
IS READY!
5
REFOLD THE
LOWER FLAP
UPWARD.
TURN THE
BASE OVER.
2
FLIP THE BASE. FOLD THE
TWO LOWER FLAPS
TOWARD THE CENTER.
3
FOLD IN HALF.
4
FOLD DOWN
THE UPPER FLAP
AS SHOWN.

n° 11

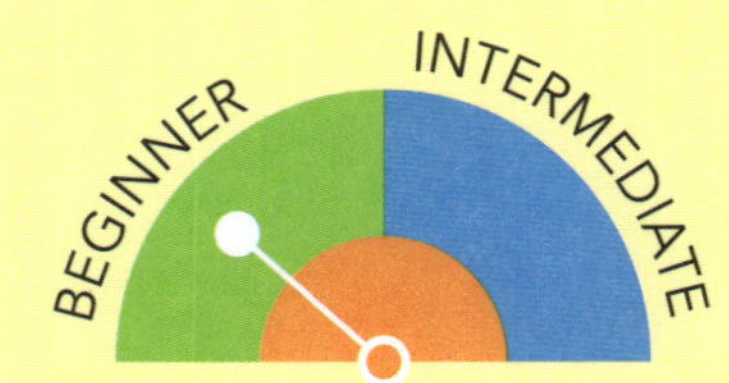

THE SWAN

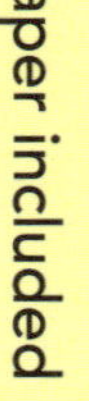

START WITH A KITE BASE.

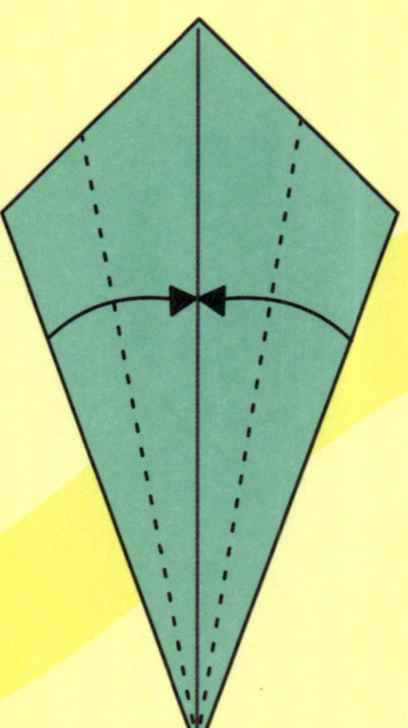

1

FLIP THE BASE.
FOLD THE TWO SIDES TO THE CENTER FOLD LINE.

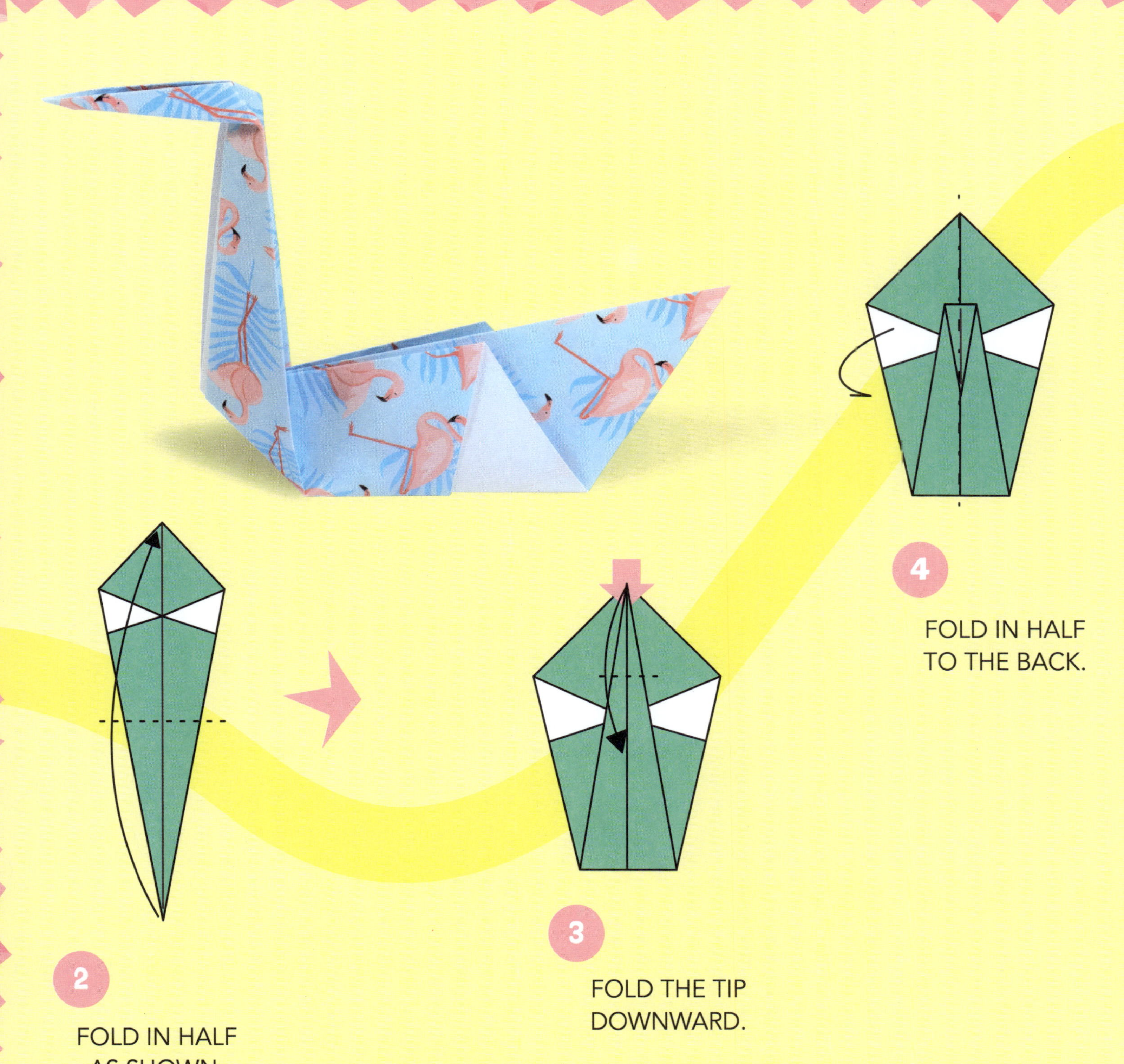

2

FOLD IN HALF
AS SHOWN.

3

FOLD THE TIP
DOWNWARD.

4

FOLD IN HALF
TO THE BACK.

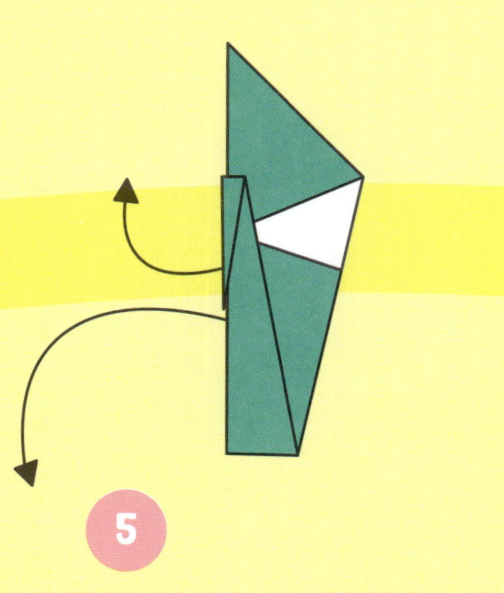

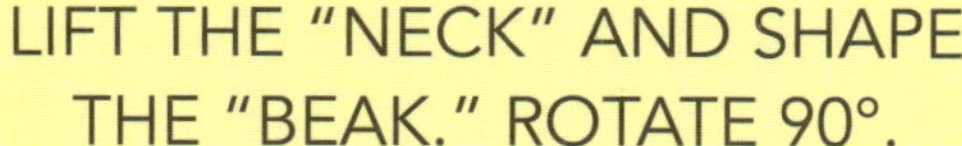

5

LIFT THE "NECK" AND SHAPE THE "BEAK." ROTATE 90°.

THE SWAN IS READY!

SOMETHING MORE:

THIS MODEL FLOATS.
USE GOOD QUALITY PAPER
WHEN MAKING IT AND THEN
TRY TO FLOAT IT ON THE WATER!

IF THE NECK ANGLE IS CORRECT,
YOU WILL SEE IT FLOAT—AT LEAST
FOR A WHILE—LIKE A REAL SWAN.

YOU CAN MAKE DIFFERENT
SIZES FOR A WHOLE FAMILY
OF SWANS!

nº 12

⇧ Paper included

THE BIRDIE

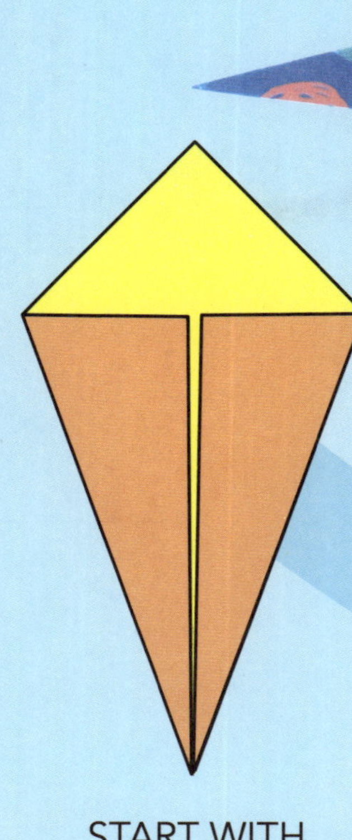

START WITH
A KITE BASE.

1

FOLD THE UPPER
TRIANGLE BACKWARD.

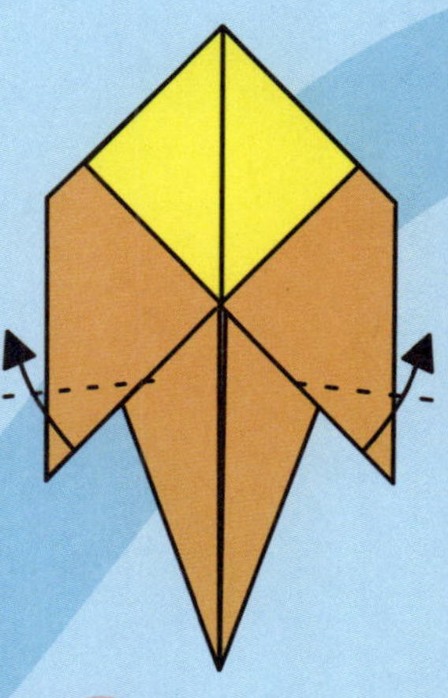

4

FOLD THE TWO CORNERS UPWARD.

WATCH THE VIDEO TO BETTER UNDERSTAND THIS STEP

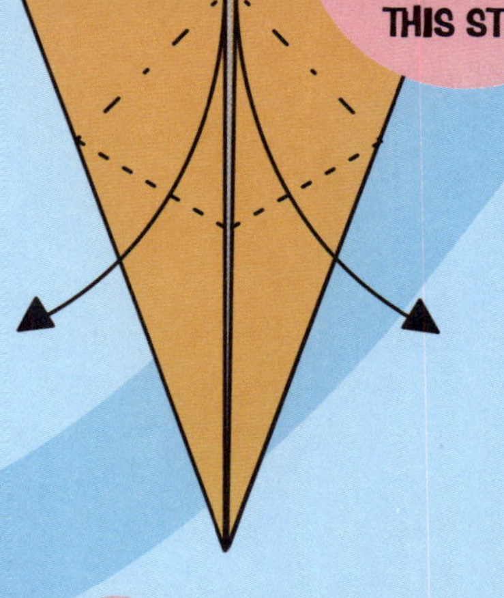

3

NOW LET'S TRY SOMETHING NEW! OPEN THE TOP TWO LAYERS AND, USING THE FOLD LINES, FLATTEN THEM DOWNWARD. THE ARROWS SHOW THE DIRECTION.

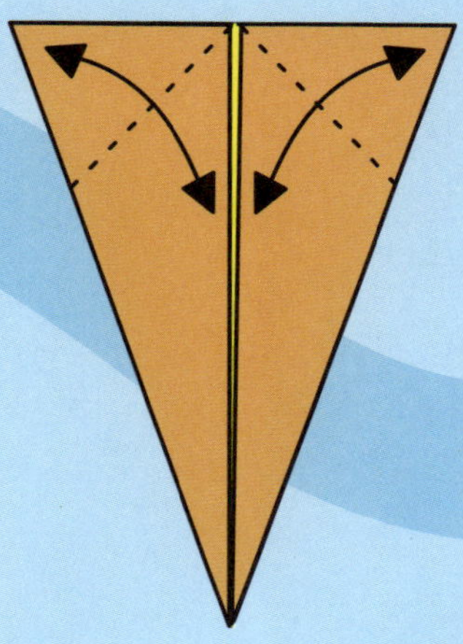

2

MOVE THE TWO UPPER CORNERS TO THE CENTER FOLD LINE. FOLD THE LINES AND OPEN AGAIN.

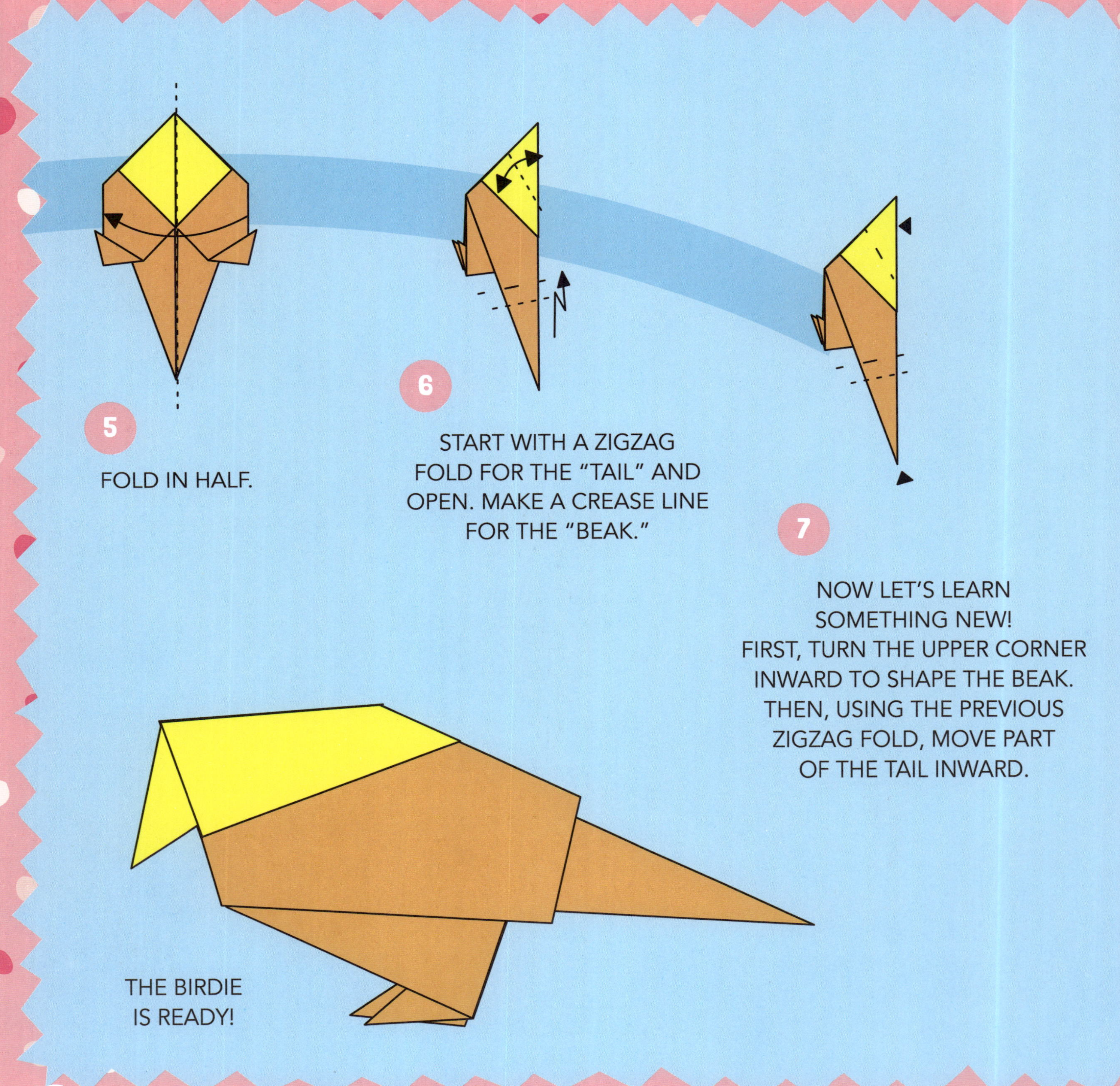
5
FOLD IN HALF.
6
START WITH A ZIGZAG
FOLD FOR THE "TAIL" AND
OPEN. MAKE A CREASE LINE
FOR THE "BEAK."
7
NOW LET'S LEARN
SOMETHING NEW!
FIRST, TURN THE UPPER CORNER
INWARD TO SHAPE THE BEAK.
THEN, USING THE PREVIOUS
ZIGZAG FOLD, MOVE PART
OF THE TAIL INWARD.
THE BIRDIE
IS READY!

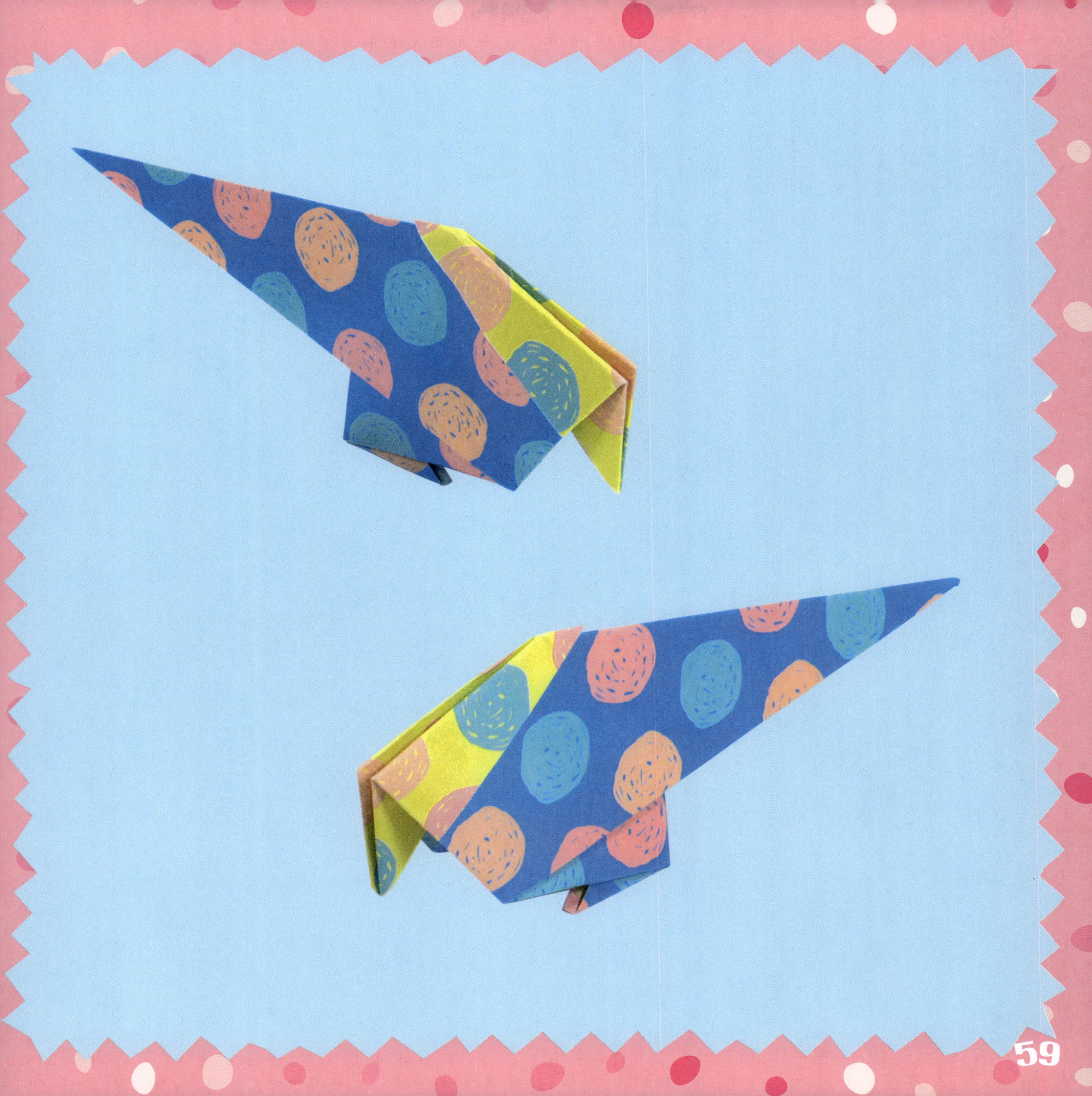

CHAPTER 5

THE DIAMOND BASE IS ALMOST THE SAME AS THE KITE BASE YOU LEARNED IN CHAPTER 4. YOU JUST HAVE TO ADD ONE MORE STEP!

WITH JUST A FEW FOLDS, YOU CAN CREATE THE TALKING CROW, AN ANIMATED ORIGAMI!

nº 13

THE DIAMOND BASE

USE A SQUARE SHEET OF PAPER

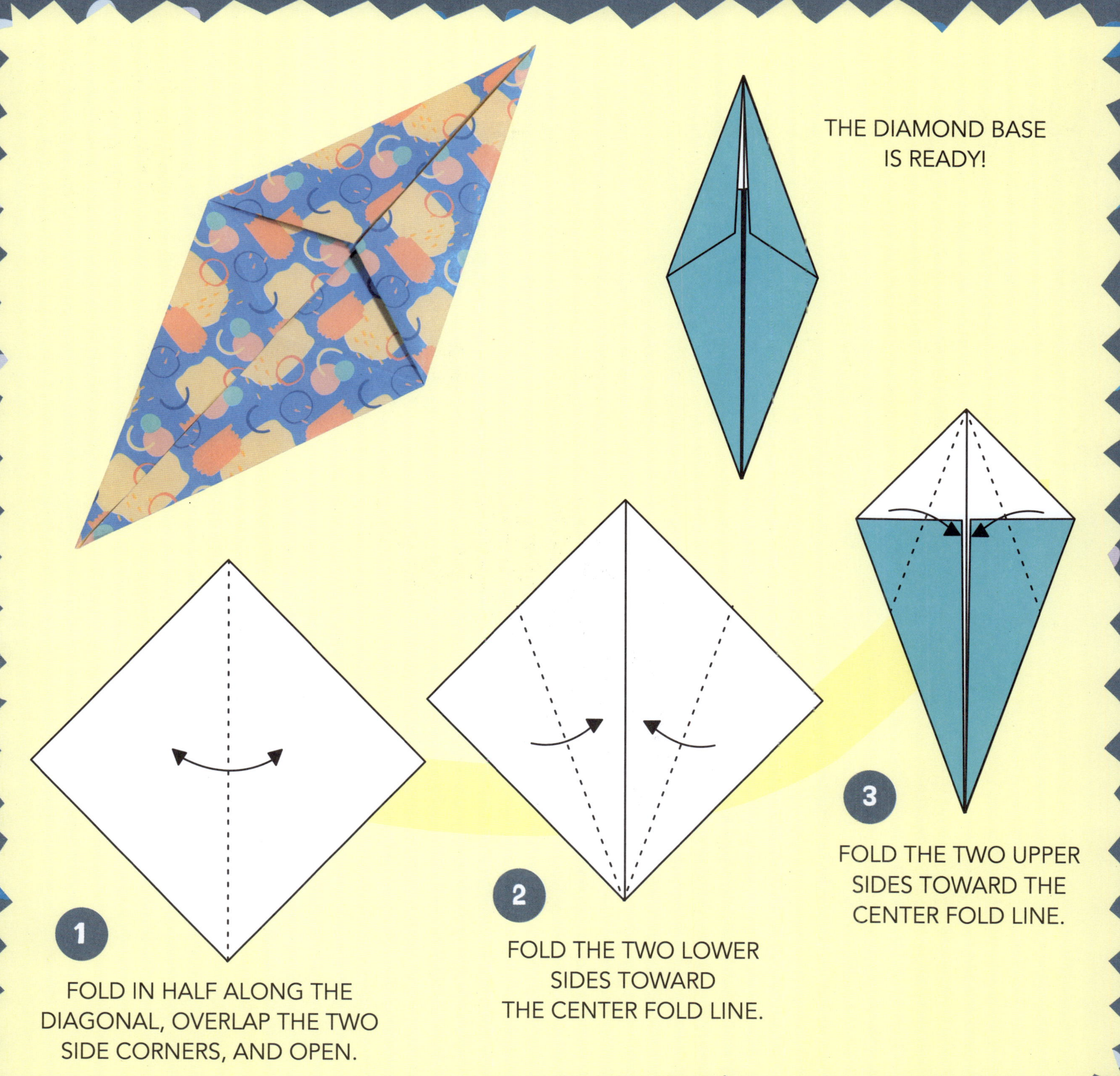
THE DIAMOND BASE
IS READY!
1
FOLD IN HALF ALONG THE
DIAGONAL, OVERLAP THE TWO
SIDE CORNERS, AND OPEN.
2
FOLD THE TWO LOWER
SIDES TOWARD
THE CENTER FOLD LINE.
3
FOLD THE TWO UPPER
SIDES TOWARD THE
CENTER FOLD LINE.

nº 14

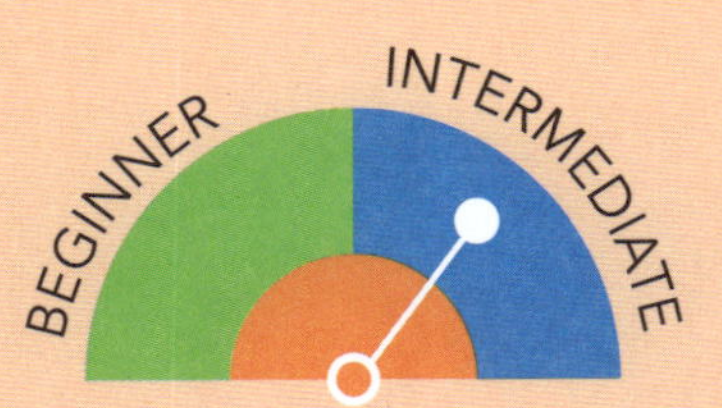

⇧ Paper included

THE TALKING CROW

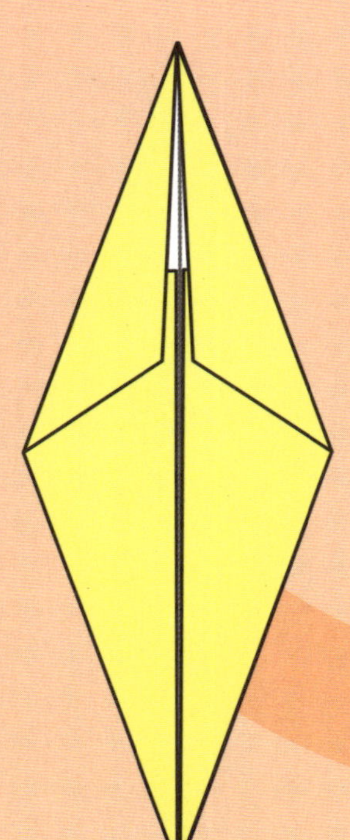

START WITH A DIAMOND BASE.

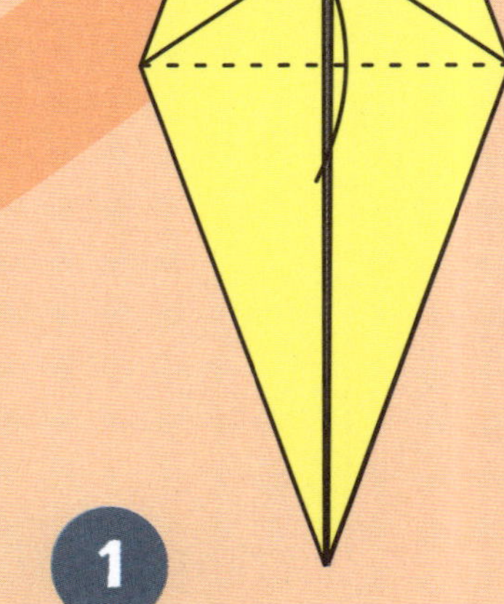

1

FOLD THE LOWER SECTION UPWARD.

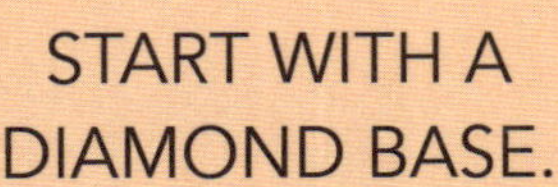

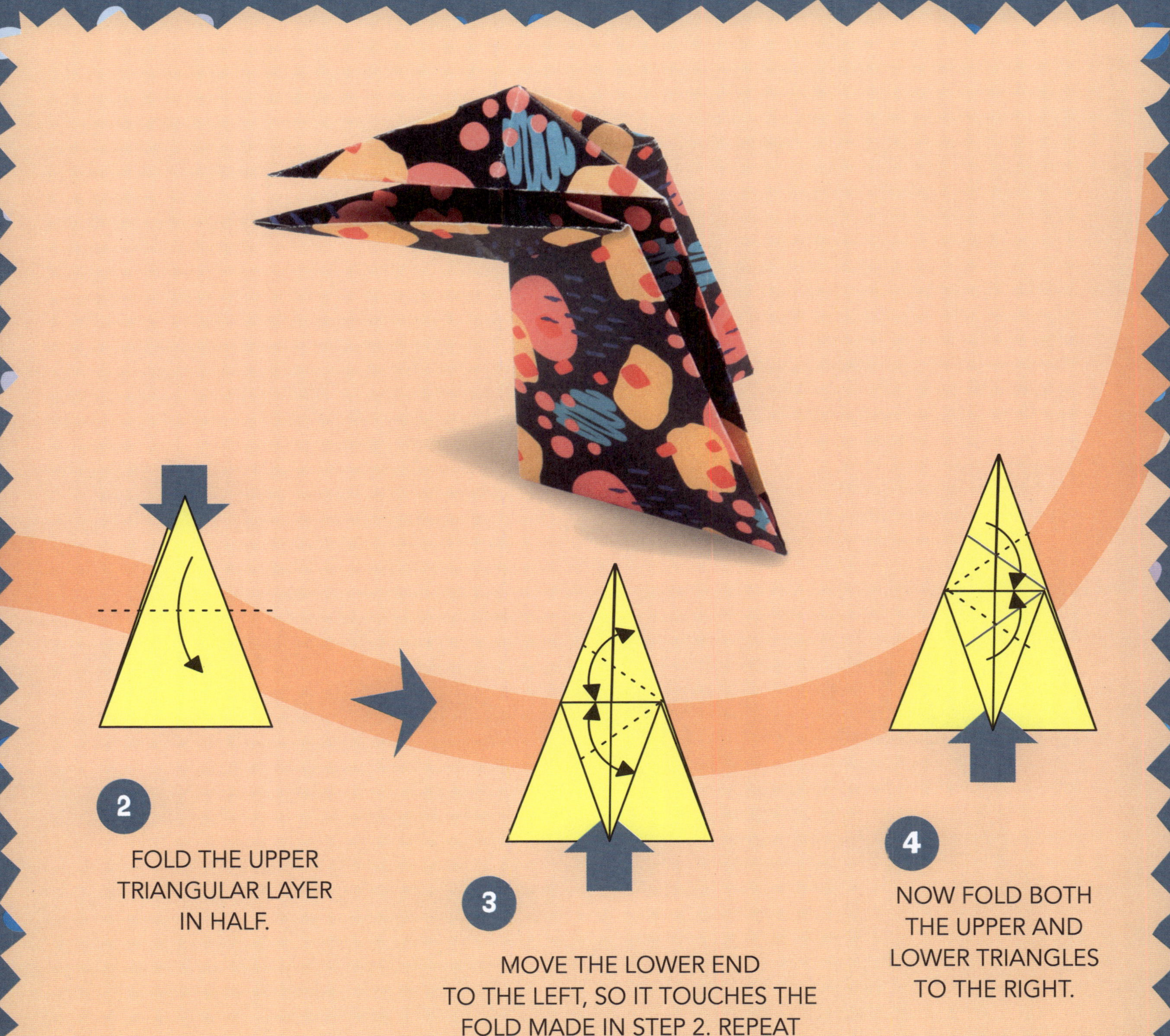

2

FOLD THE UPPER TRIANGULAR LAYER IN HALF.

3

MOVE THE LOWER END TO THE LEFT, SO IT TOUCHES THE FOLD MADE IN STEP 2. REPEAT ON THE UPPER TRIANGLE.

4

NOW FOLD BOTH THE UPPER AND LOWER TRIANGLES TO THE RIGHT.

5

FOLD BACK THE RIGHT HALF. THE FOLD LINES MADE IN PREVIOUS STEPS WILL HELP YOU SHAPE THE "BEAK" (SEE STEP 5A).

5a

SOMETIMES THE IMAGES SHOW INTERMEDIATE STEPS TO BETTER ILLUSTRATE HOW EACH FOLD IS MADE.

THE TALKING CROW IS READY!

TO MOVE IT:

PUT YOUR FINGERS ON THE POINTS MARKED BY THE RED DOTS.

AS YOU MOVE THE PARTS IN THE DIRECTION SHOWN BY THE ARROWS, THE BEAK OPENS AND CLOSES AS IF THE CROW WERE TALKING!

CHAPTER 6

YOU CAN EASILY GUESS THAT THE FISH BASE OWES ITS NAME TO THE MANY SEA CREATURES YOU CAN CREATE BY FOLDING IT IN DIFFERENT WAYS.

n° 15

THE FISH BASE

Paper included

USE A SQUARE SHEET OF PAPER

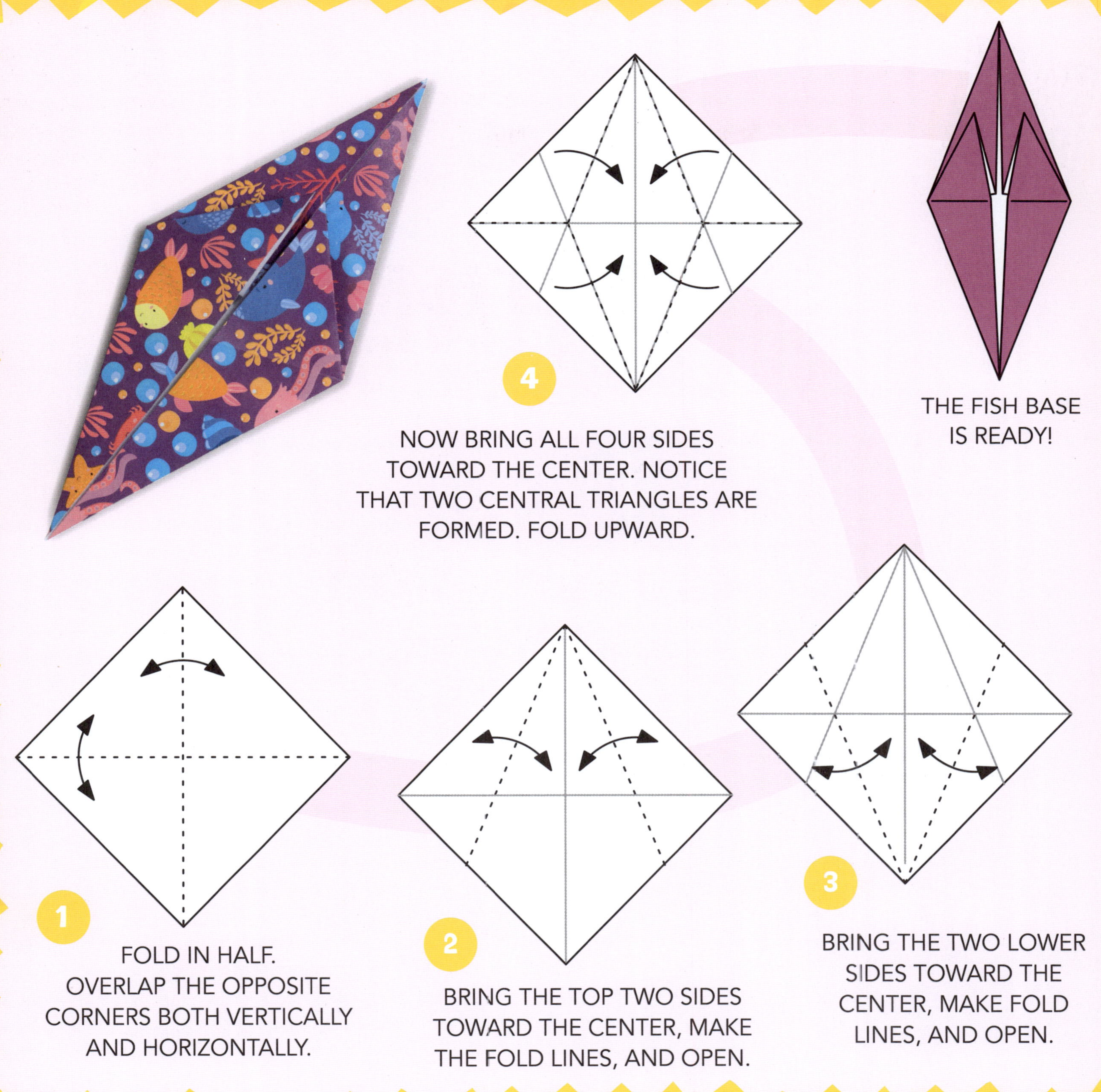
4
NOW BRING ALL FOUR SIDES TOWARD THE CENTER. NOTICE THAT TWO CENTRAL TRIANGLES ARE FORMED. FOLD UPWARD.
THE FISH BASE IS READY!
1
FOLD IN HALF. OVERLAP THE OPPOSITE CORNERS BOTH VERTICALLY AND HORIZONTALLY.
2
BRING THE TOP TWO SIDES TOWARD THE CENTER, MAKE THE FOLD LINES, AND OPEN.
3
BRING THE TWO LOWER SIDES TOWARD THE CENTER, MAKE FOLD LINES, AND OPEN.

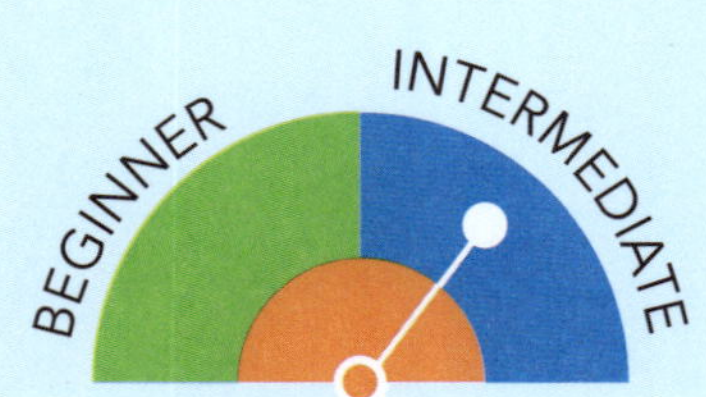

nº 16

THE WHALE

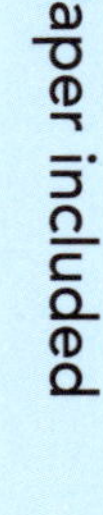

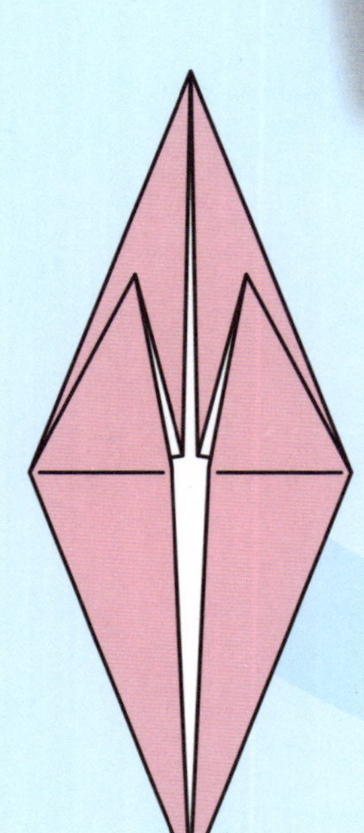

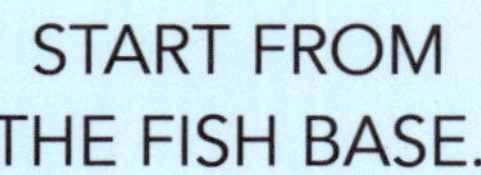

START FROM THE FISH BASE.

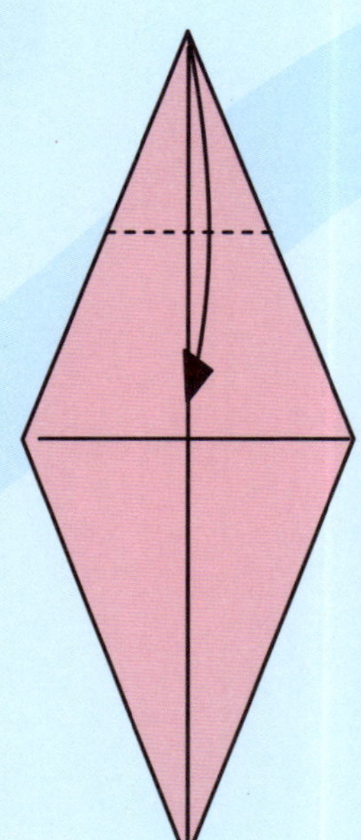

1

FLIP THE BASE.
FOLD THE TOP CORNER TOWARD THE CENTER.

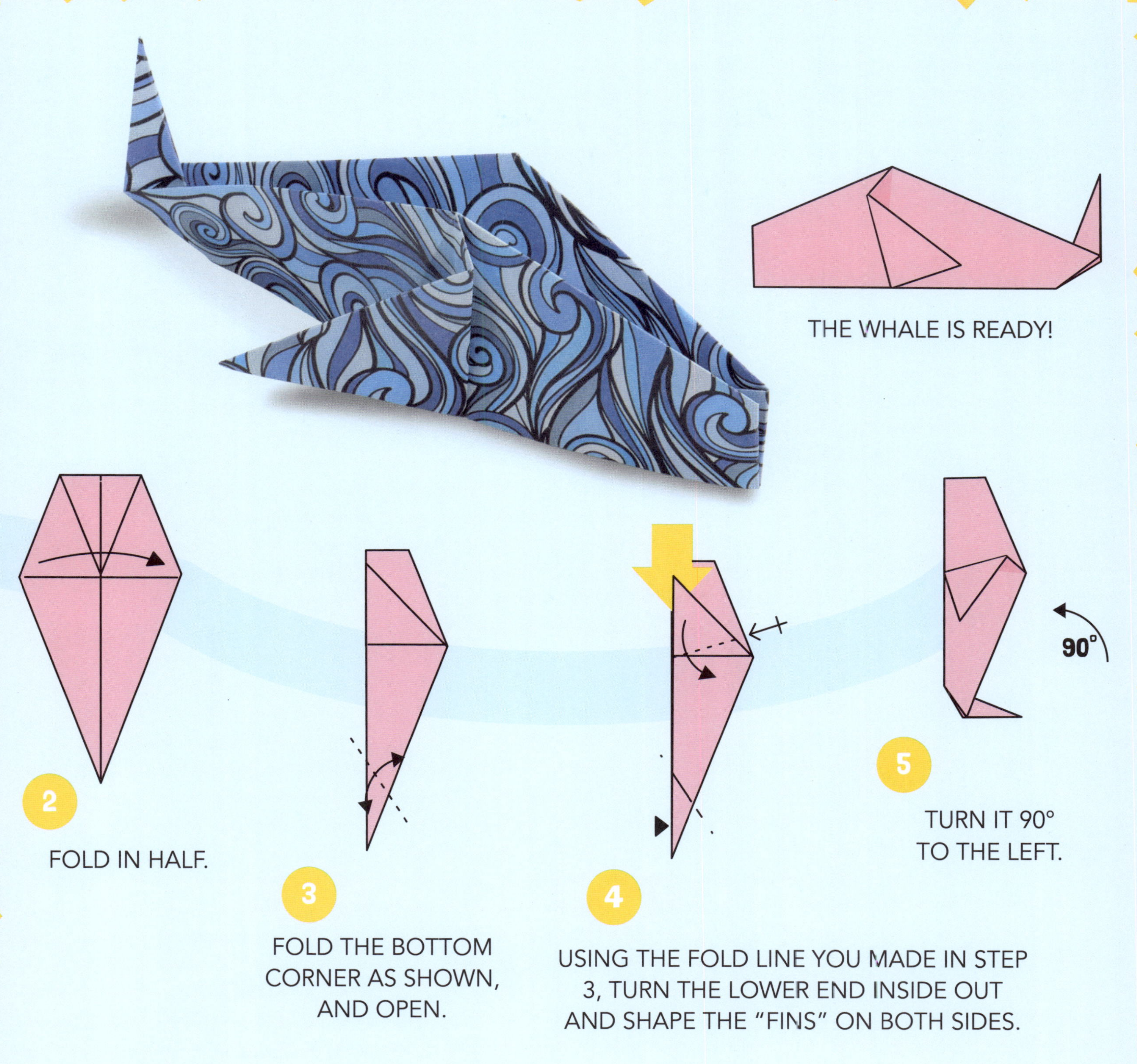
THE WHALE IS READY!
2
FOLD IN HALF.
3
FOLD THE BOTTOM CORNER AS SHOWN, AND OPEN.
4
USING THE FOLD LINE YOU MADE IN STEP 3, TURN THE LOWER END INSIDE OUT AND SHAPE THE "FINS" ON BOTH SIDES.
90°
5
TURN IT 90° TO THE LEFT.

n° 17

THE SEAL

Paper included

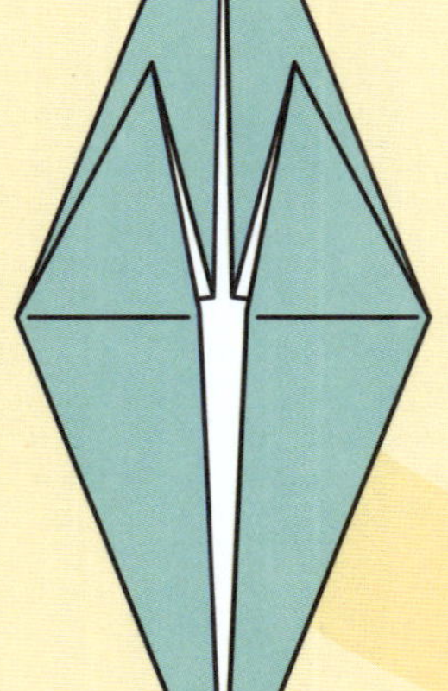

START FROM THE FISH BASE.

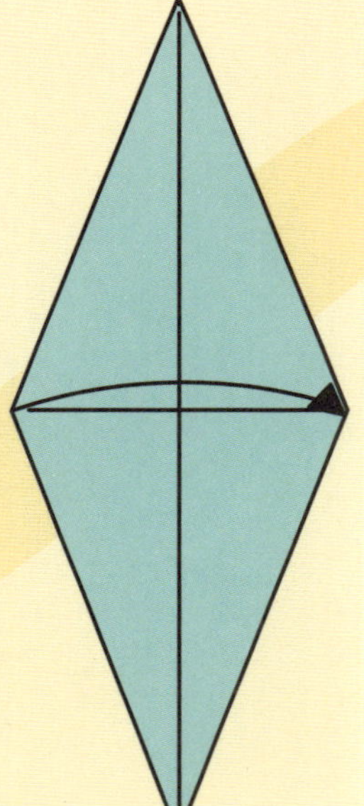

1

FLIP THE BASE. FOLD IN HALF. REPEAT ON THE OTHER SIDE.

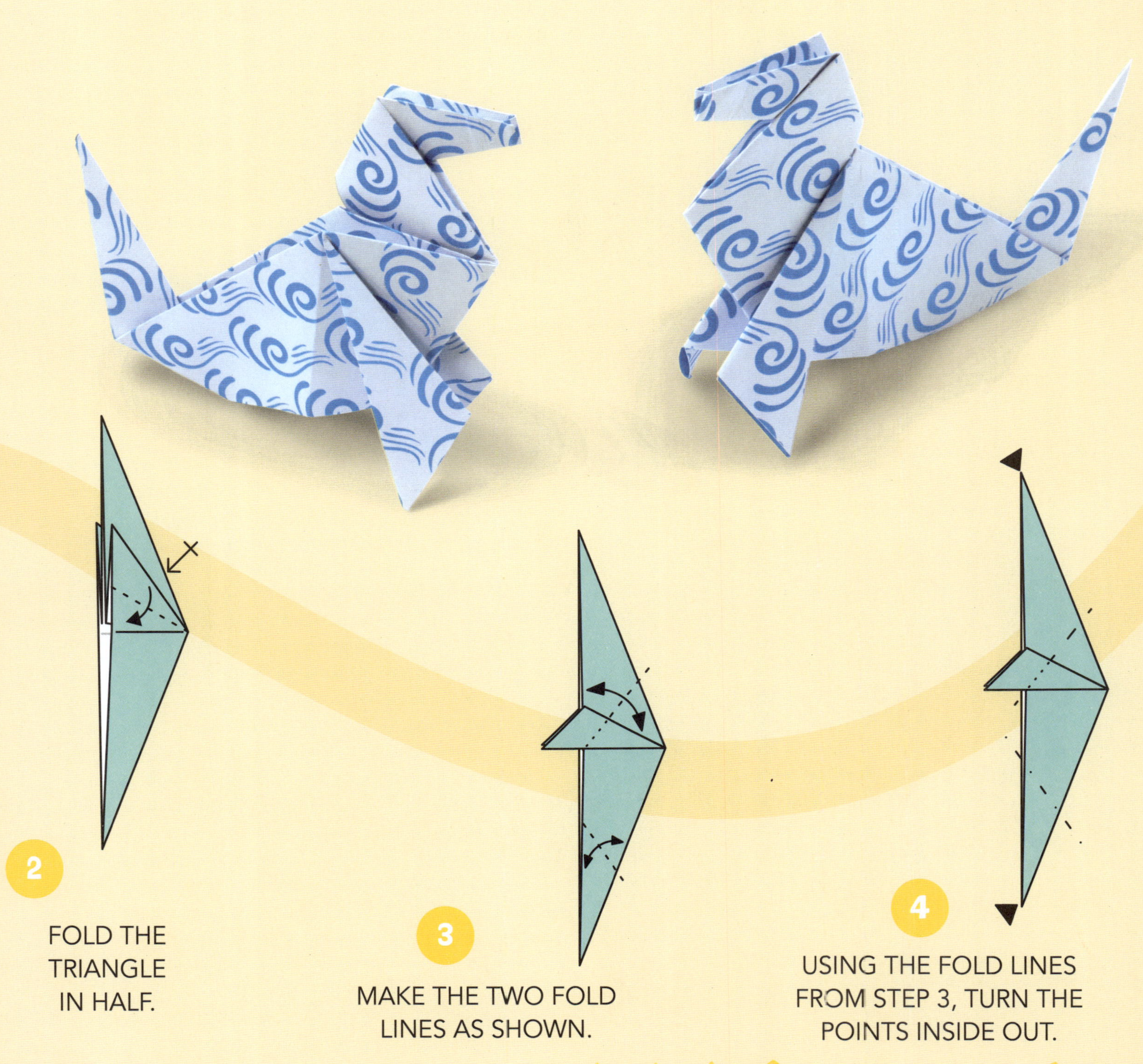

2

FOLD THE TRIANGLE IN HALF.

3

MAKE THE TWO FOLD LINES AS SHOWN.

4

USING THE FOLD LINES FROM STEP 3, TURN THE POINTS INSIDE OUT.

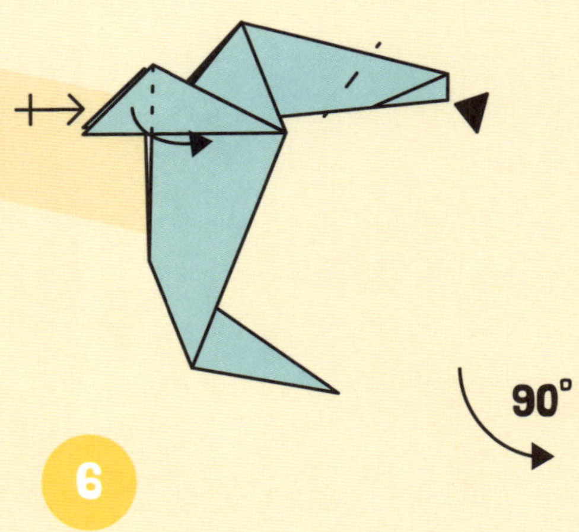

5

NOW LET'S LEARN
SOMETHING NEW!
TURN THE TIP INSIDE OUT.

6

TURN THE "HEAD"
INWARD AND FORM THE
"FINS" ON BOTH SIDES.

TURN IT 90° TO THE LEFT.

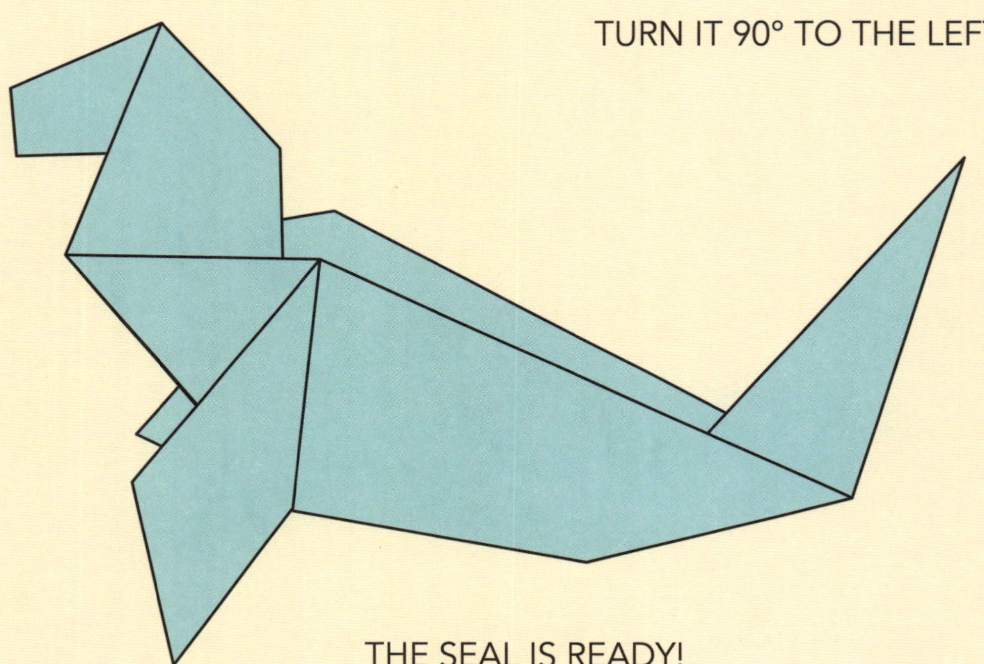

THE SEAL IS READY!

CHAPTER 7

IT MAY SEEM STRANGE, BUT YOU'VE PROBABLY DONE IT HUNDREDS OF TIMES: THE INSTINCT TO FOLD A SHEET OF PAPER IN HALF WHEN YOU HOLD IT IN YOUR HANDS.

EVEN WITHOUT THINKING, FROM THAT SIMPLE FOLD, YOU CAN CREATE A LEAPING FROG!

nº 18

THE BOOK BASE

Paper included

USE A SQUARE SHEET OF PAPER

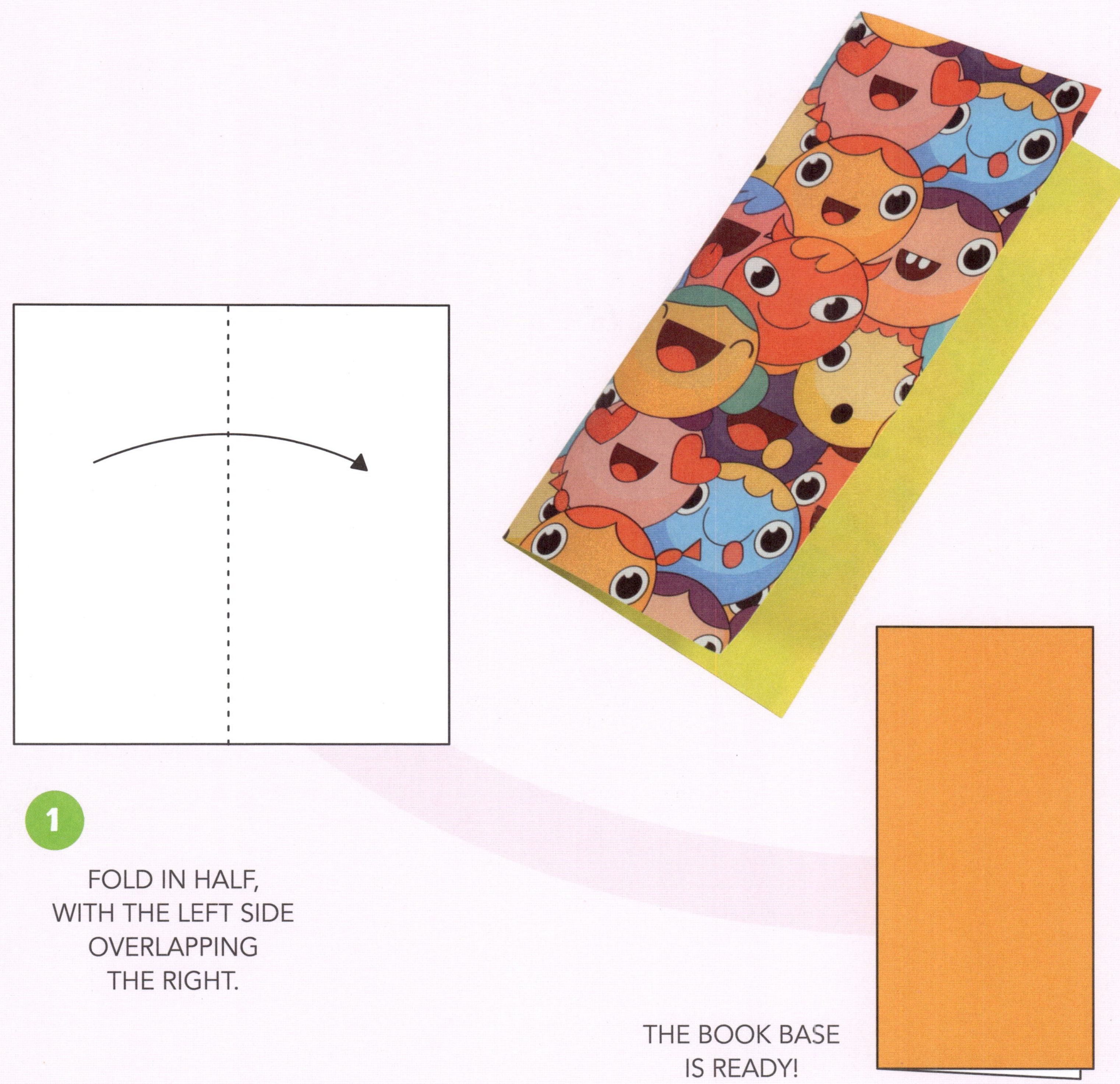

1

FOLD IN HALF, WITH THE LEFT SIDE OVERLAPPING THE RIGHT.

THE BOOK BASE IS READY!

nº 19

THE JUMPING FROG

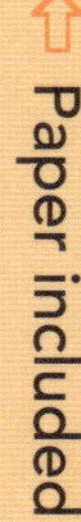

Paper included

START WITH A BOOK BASE.

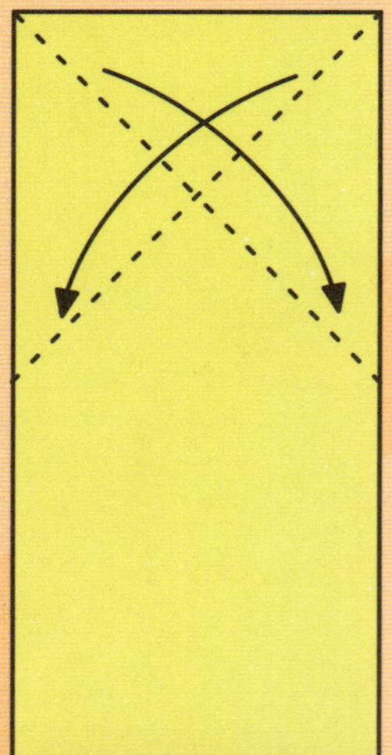

1

FOLD THE TOP SIDE DIAGONALLY IN BOTH DIRECTIONS, THEN OPEN.

2
FOLD BACK THE TOP SIDE FROM THE POINT WHERE THE TWO FOLD LINES INTERSECT, AND OPEN.
3
USING THE FOLD LINES FROM THE PREVIOUS STEPS, OPEN AND FLATTEN DOWNWARD TO FORM A TRIANGLE.
4
FOLD THE TWO CORNERS AT THE BASE OF THE TRIANGLE TOWARD THE CENTER.

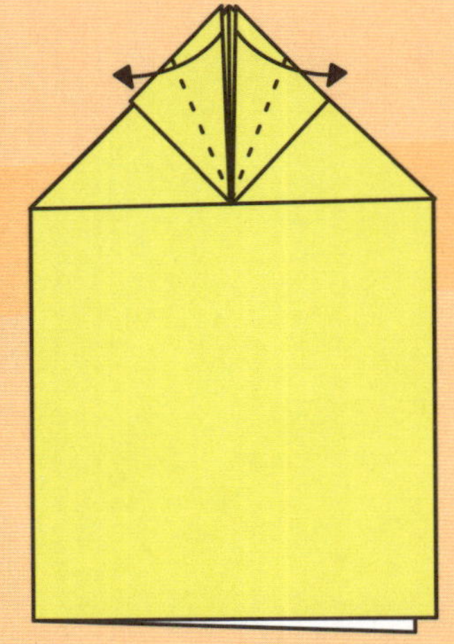

5

UNFOLD THE TWO TOP ENDS OUTWARD.

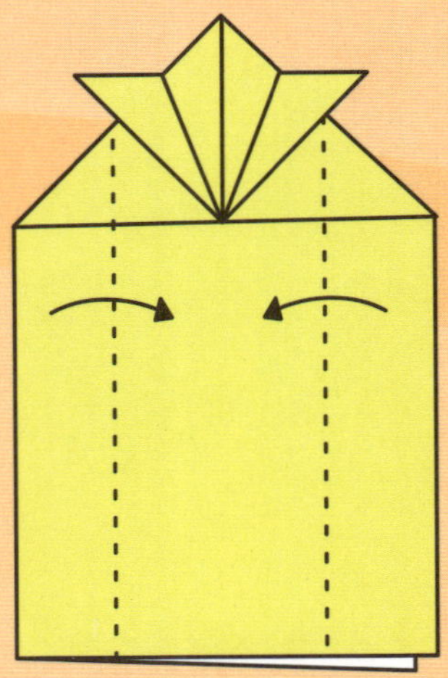

6

FOLD THE TWO SIDES TOWARD THE CENTER.

7

FOLD THE BOTTOM SECTION UPWARD UNTIL IT TOUCHES THE BOTTOM EDGE OF THE TRIANGLES.

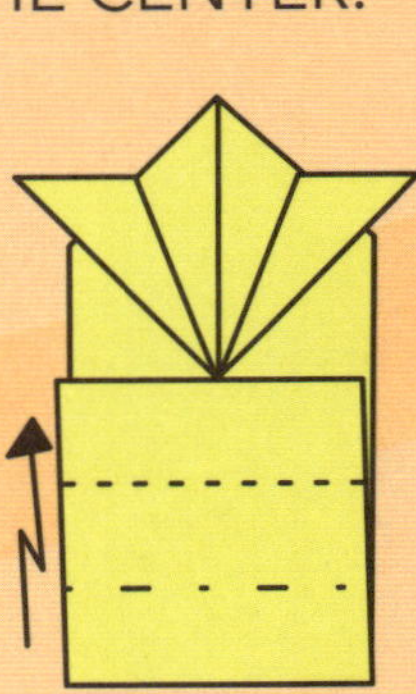

8

MAKE THE ZIGZAG FOLD AS SHOWN. FLIP THE MODEL OVER.

THE JUMPING FROG IS READY!

TO MOVE IT:

PRESS YOUR FINGER ON THE FROG'S BACK AND LET IT GO TO MAKE IT JUMP!

Improve your technique for better results

To help you master the folds in this book, each project contains a QR code at the top of the first page that will bring you to an instructional video.

These videos show the movements needed, and you can replay them or focus on tricky steps as many times as you need. Plus, YouTube lets you slow down the playback, which is great when you are trying to make the more challenging origami models.

I also recommend exploring other books once you've got the basics down. As your curiosity grows, you'll want to dive deeper into the vast world of origami. There are so many techniques and applications to discover, and exploring them will help you grow in this art.

Learning to make origami takes patience and discipline, but the rewards are worth it. Not only will your concentration and attention span improve, but you'll also find that it positively impacts many other areas of your life.

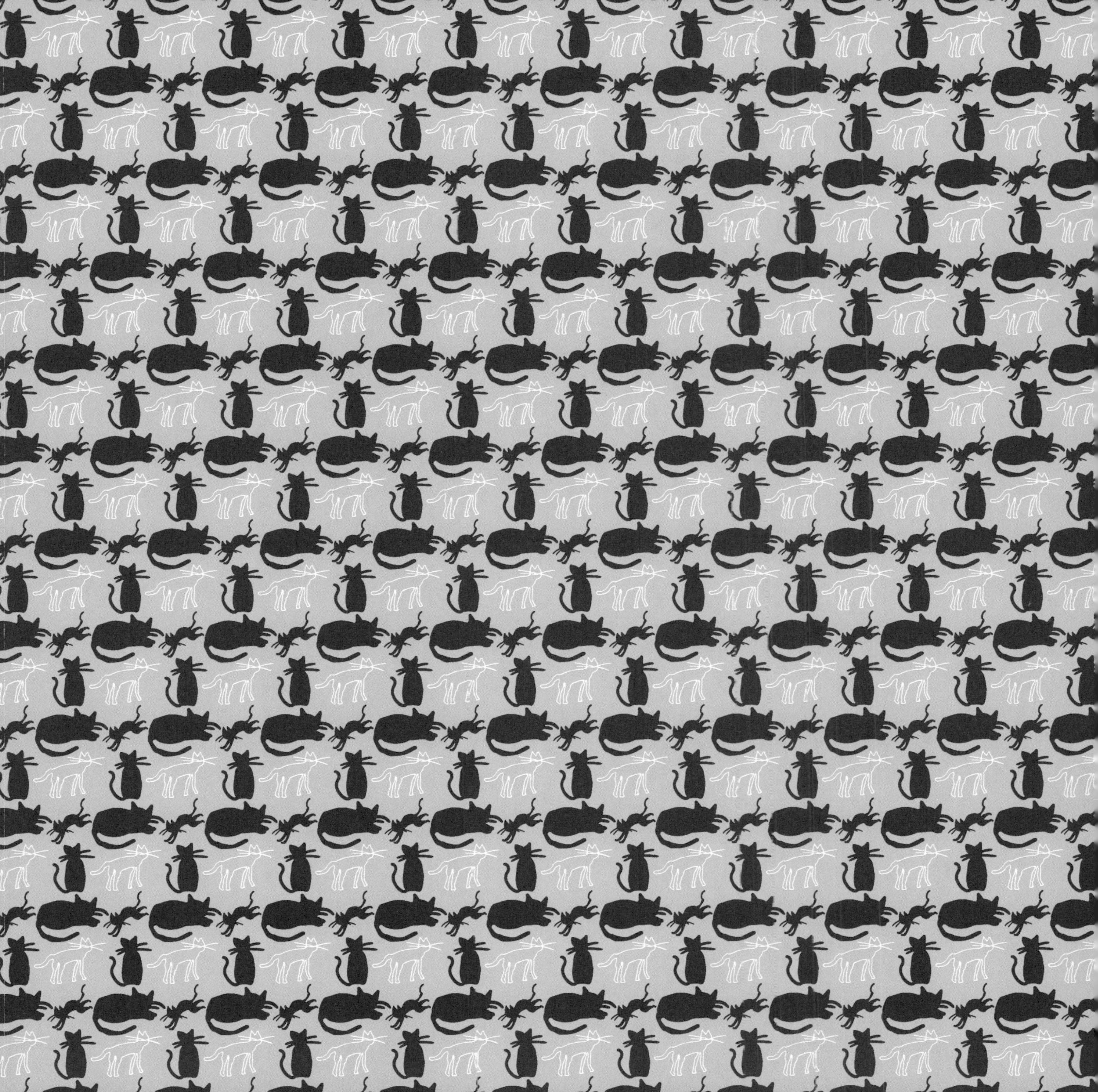

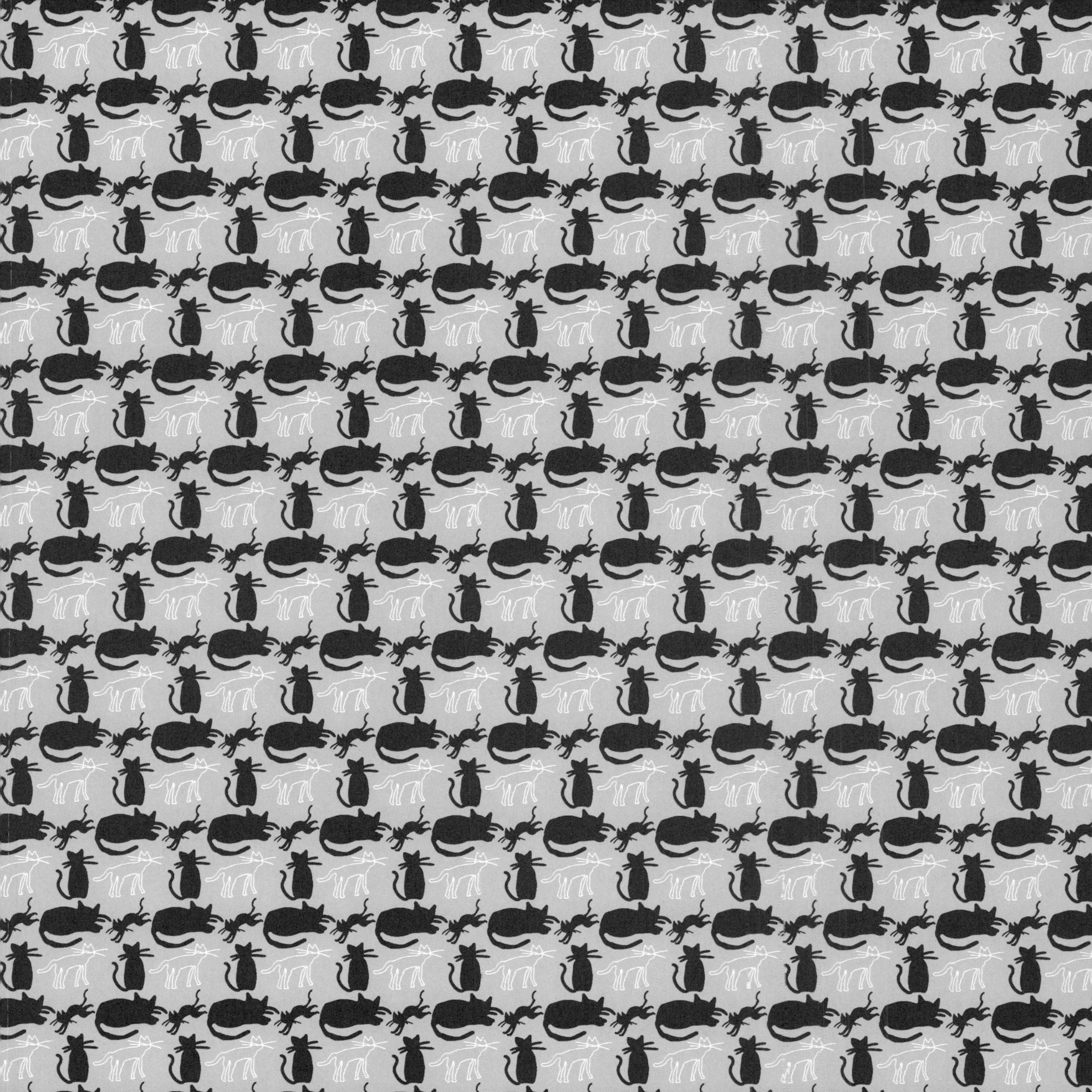

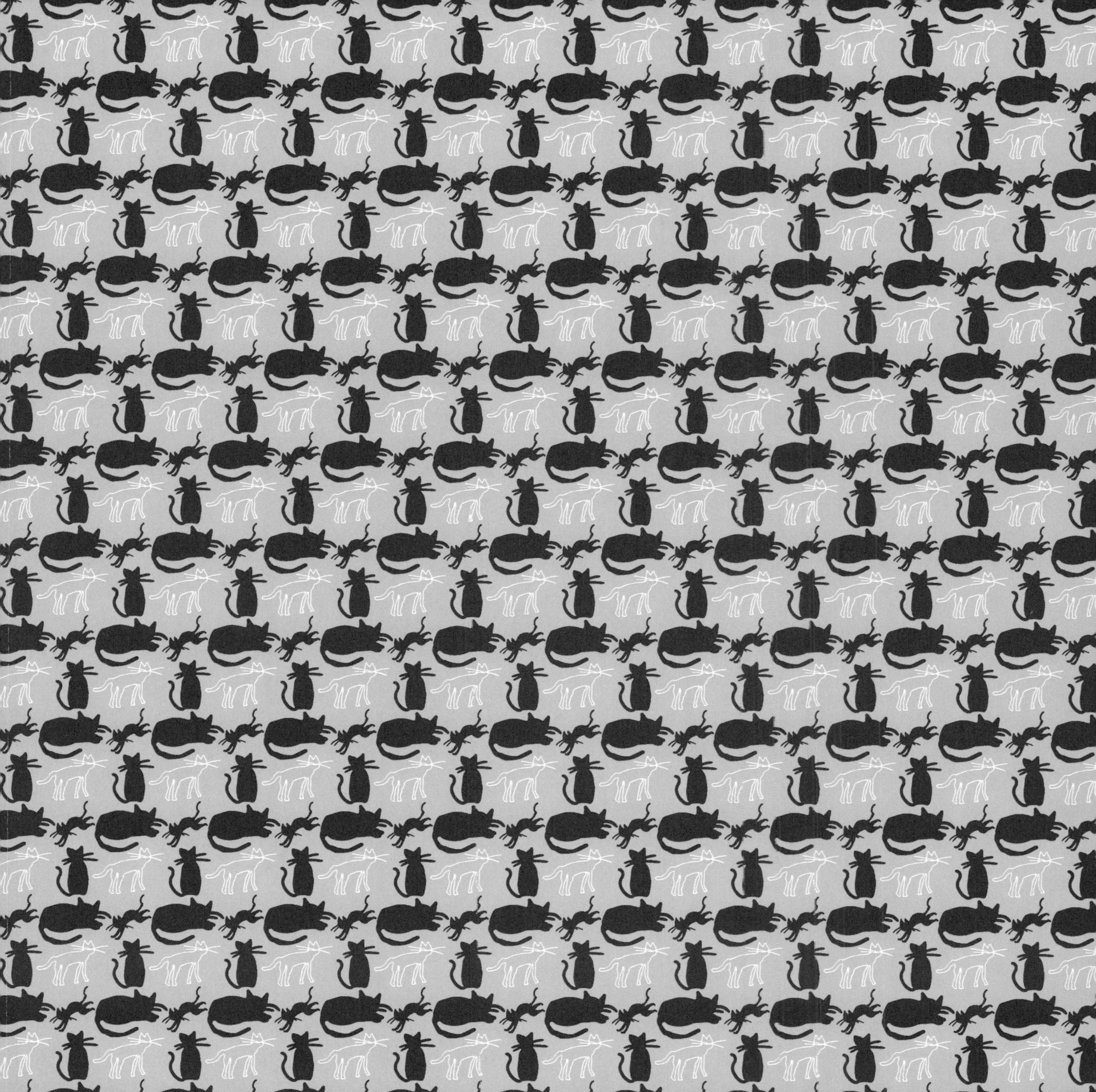

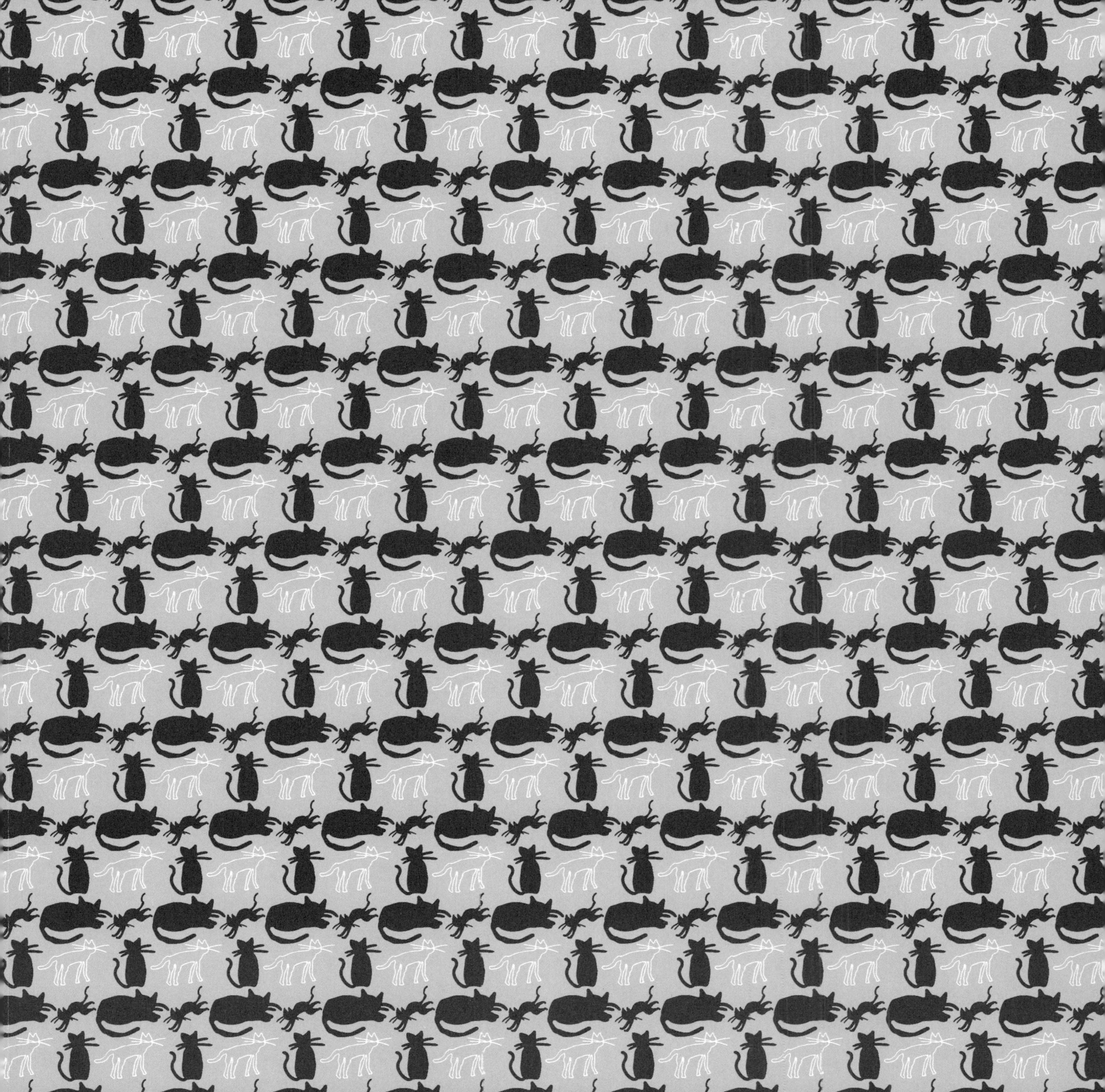